DEATH
A New Perspective on the Phenomena of Disease and Dying

DEATH

A New Perspective on the Phenomena of Disease and Dying

Drs. M.L. Kothari and L.A. Mehta

Marion Boyars . London . New York

First Published in Great Britain and in the United States 1986 by
Marion Boyars Publishers
24 Lacy Road, London SW15 1NL.
262 West 22nd Street, New York, N.Y. 10011

Distributed in the United States by
The Scribner Book Companies, Inc.

Distributed in Canada by
Collier Macmillan Canada Inc.

Distributed in Australia by
Wild and Woolley Pty Ltd.
16 Darghan Street,
Glebe, NSW 2037

Distributed in New Zealand by
Benton Ross Ltd.
PO Box 33055, Takapuna, Auckland 9.

© Kothari and Mehta 1986

All rights reserved.

No part of this publication may be reproduced, stored in a retrieval system or transmitted in any form, or by any means, electronic, mechanical, photocopying, recording or otherwise except brief extracts for the purposes of review, without the prior permission of the publishers.

Any paperback edition of this book whether published simultaneously with, or subsequent to, the casebound edition is sold subject to the condition that it shall not, by way of trade be lent, resold, hired out or otherwise disposed of without the publishers' consent, in any form of binding other than that in which it was published.

British Library Cataloguing in Publication Data

Kothari, Manu L.
   Death: a new perspective on the phenomena of disease
   and dying.
   1. Death
   I. Title II. Mehta, Lopa A.
   128'.5 BD444

Library of Congress Cataloging in Publication Data

Kothari, M.L. (Manu L.)
   Death, a new perspective on the the phenomena of disease
   and dying.
   Bibliography: p.
   Includes indexes.
   1. Terminal care—Psychological aspects. 2. Death—
   Psychological aspects. 3. Sick—Psychology. I. Mehta,
L.A. (Lopa A.) II. Title.
R726.8.K68 1986   616.07'8   85-17056

ISBN 0-7145-2846-3 Cloth

Typeset by Essex Photo Set, Rayleigh, Essex, England
Printed and bound in Great Britain by
Biddles Ltd, Guildford and King's Lynn

By the same authors

CANCER:
Myths and Realities of Cause and Cure

Nothing in life is to be feared.
It's only to be understood.

Marie Curie

Dedicated to Dr. Dipak L. Kothari (1947–1977)
MS, MD
Orthopaedic Surgeon
Bombay and New Jersey
and to
Romal M Kothari (1973–1985)

Memento Mori

Contents

Acknowledgements		13
Preface		15
Chapter 1	Understanding Disease and Death	18
Chapter 2	The Democracy of Disease	22
Chapter 3	The Democracy of Death	33
Chapter 4	Death: Design and Definition	44
Chapter 5	The Trans-science Aspects of Disease and Death	55
Chapter 6	The Trans-technique Aspects of Disease and Death	66
Chapter 7	The Dictates of the Nature of Disease and Death	78
Chapter 8	Reverence for Death is Reverence for Life	91
Chapter 9	Life and Death: Here and Now	102
Chapter 10	Life and Death: Before and Beyond	113
Bibliography		119
Name Index		123
Subject Index		125

Acknowledgements

Let noble thoughts come to us from all sides.

Rigveda

The one teacher that a medical student and a doctor can forever learn from is a patient – the very *raison d'être* of the art and the science of medicine. A doctor does *not* treat a patient; he interacts with the patient to enlighten himself and to help the patient. We are deeply grateful to all the diseased fellow beings we have had the privilege to interact with, for the insight they have given us into health, disease, recovery from disease, dying, and death.

Jayanthi Mani, Asmita Mehta, Mayur Mehta, Dr. Rajesh Parikh, Dr. Sunil Pandya and Dr. S.M. Bhatnagar have critically evaluated the style and the substance of the book. Their compassionate and critical perusal has enabled us to simplify, abbreviate, or amplify the text making it both more comprehensible and readable.

Swami Suddhabodhananda, Vasant Shukla, Harindra Dave and Ghanshyam Desai provided us access to the Indian Scriptures, the etymology of Sanskrit words, and a wider understanding of the concept of the Upanishads.

Dr. Jyoti Kothari, L.P. Kothari, Vatsal Kothari, A.J. Mehta, Ramila Bhatt, Mahesh Bhatt, Rusi Engineer, Claude Alvares, Ashis Nandy, Pritish Nandy, Nikhil Lakshman, Dr. J.K. Bhatt, Dr. Rupin Shah, Chandrakant Shah, Hemang Shah, Raj Parab, Ramesh Parab, Chandrika Pani, Dr. N. Laxminayana, David de Souza, Prof. M.N. Pandia and Dr. Sulbha Punekar, and the members of our families have all along been encouraging and helpful. We owe a great deal to their kindness and love.

It has been a pleasure to have Mr. Keshav Godhia as a co-worker. All that we write passes through his hands to come out as a typescript. Immaculateness is his; the errors are ours.

Marion Boyars has urged us to be ourselves – heretical here, scientific there – encouraging us, through her readings of previous drafts to emphasize Eastern thought. The tacit contract of mutual patience between her and ourselves has been rewarding in more than one way.

Preface

> But it is now time to depart, – for me to die, for you to live. But which of us is going to a better state is unknown to everyone but God.
>
> *Socrates*

On a rainy evening on October 7, 1977, we were arranging the slides for a talk on October 10. The theme of the presentation was an integrative concept of death's non-dependence on disease and its impartial but inexorable sway on mankind. At that time, it was early morning at Fort Lee, New Jersey. Dipak – Dr. Kothari's brother – had his morning tea, and then stretched himself out on the bed for a while, and died. He had had a massive heart attack. His wife Poorvi returned in the afternoon to find Dipak lying most peacefully in bed.

Dipak was a tall, handsome person, athletically built and inclined. He had had neither diabetes nor high blood pressure, nor excess weight – none of the 'risk' factors. He belonged to a family of nonagenarians where, from among 20 such adults, nobody has had even anginal pain. Yet Dipak, against every cardiologic claim to predisposing factors, died of coronary artery occlusion.

For Dr. Kothari, with whom Dipak grew from school days through postgraduation, this was a rude shock. However, the head consoled the grieving heart, persistently driving home the point that death's mathematics does its task governed solely by Pascalian probabilities, irreverent in the face of medical attempts at prevention, diagnosis and treatment. We have lived with Dipak's death and with the understanding of its significance in the overall working of Nature. What appears as cruelly unjust, chaotic and disorderly at the individual and family level, is but a part of the impartial, fully just, greater order.

DEATH

Mankind fears disease and dreads death – an attitude promoted over the centuries by medical men. However, what helped us understand Dipak's death, we thought, could stand by many others. And hence this book.

We have found that the biological and medical data on death is highly comprehensible. Death emerges not as some accidental, unfortunate, macabre freak of Nature, but as a pristine, vital and co-ordinated herd or group function. The greek root *Demos;* meaning people, lies at the heart of democracy. Disease – cancer, heart attack, diabetes, and so on – and death are democratic being biologically of the people, governed by the people, and we might accept in good cheer, exercised for the people. Such a humane approach to disease and death allows us to delve into the very meaning of man's life and of man's death through a synthesis of science, philosophy, and religion.

Indian scriptures have revered death as the great, impartial ruler in whose reign the king and the commoner, the physician and the patient, the rich and the poor, the male and the female, the aged and the young, all are treated alike. Such a view of death allows one to befriend death and not be afraid of it, allows one to live every moment of life and not to die a thousand deaths before the climactic moment.

Were this book to bear a title in an Indian language, it would have been called *Mrutyu Upanishad* or *Death Upanishad*. The term Upanishad comes from *upa* (near to) *ni-shad* (to sit) meaning "sitting down near" for a *tête-à-tête* to admire, appreciate, comprehend many a thing, mundane or mighty. The attendant informality has a built-in respect for the lay person's ability to understand what is shunned as complex by the learned. The mood of uninhibited inquiry, the Upanishadic spirit, is pregnant with the possibility of distilling wisdom through common sense. The humility of sitting child-like before some seemingly scary realities gives one the clarity of vision to welcome the inevitable, and benefit therefrom, unclouded by the current scientific hubris and the medical world's blind optimism.

Death accepts *what is, is right,* and then proceeds to present a perspective that has no quarrel either with human aspirations or

PREFACE

with some hard facts. An underlying order governing disease and death unfolds itself, giving the patient and the physician, the dying and the near ones a sense of direction and purpose that hitherto has not existed. *Death* is an exercise in natural philosophy, wherein science vindicates the philosophic and religious approach to disease and death.

Manu Kothari
Lopa Mehta

CHAPTER 1   Understanding Disease and Death

> Man knows that things die. He witnesses their deaths and sometimes even executes them. These traumatic deaths are easy to understand. A complex living system is quickly and radically destroyed, and it ceases functioning. Natural death, the main subject of this article, is much more difficult to grasp.
>
> *The New Encyclopaedia Britannica*

These are the years of the *thanatologic imperative:* Death must be understood. Death must be discussed as an everyday topic. Death must be accepted. Death must be rationalized. But how? A simplified biologic approach to human disease and death can help achieve the current thanatologic aim of making people understand, and accept, death as but the obverse side of a coin called life.

About death, mankind seems curiously schizophrenic. On the one hand, man exalts himself as the only one, alone of all living creatures, to be privileged to know and conceive of his death as a *must* in the double sense – that it is inevitable and without exception. On the other hand, man, once again the only one among all animals, resents, dreads, and fights this unexceptionable inevitability with such paranoic vigour that death has been rendered in our time obscene.

The genesis of this schizophrenia is likely to be rooted in the recently discovered, natural dichotomy in man's cerebral hemispheres: His "right brain", artistic, imaginative, poetic, wiser, older-in-age, and intuitive in its perception of the reality, could have had no problem understanding, and thus even accepting, death as inevitable and without exception. The "left brain", wedded to the dictates of reason, and the urge to Promethean

UNDERSTANDING DISEASE AND DEATH

action, has not yet been able to assign death and its peremptoriness a place in the logical scheme of things. This is the age of the dominance of man's "left brain", by its mighty material achievements, by its felicity of overpowering verbiage, and most of all by its ability, to foster unreason by the misuse of reason. Mankind truly is caught between its two minds. The "right brain" has accepted death long ago; the left is still struggling to find the necessary scheme and the parlance to do so. This book is addressed basically to man's "left brain", his left cerebral hemisphere – to provide it with a comprehensible scheme and language to enable it to understand death in its bio-logical entirety.

What is to be understood?

Medical science has been advancing one disease or another as *the* cause of death. Causability of death by disease, so the medical logic goes, presupposes its curability – by the prevention or the cure of disease. Modern medicine, however, couldn't have been more wrong than in its naive but enduring assumption that disease causes death. Altogether, death has little to do with health and sickness; it uses them for its ends.

Disease and death, in fact, are inherent components of man's development, are governed by time and regulated by the herd, behave independently of each other and, in essence, are causally unrelated, death by itself being a programmed normal function performed by a living being. Individual development which begins at conception is neither completed in the womb nor concluded at birth; it goes on throughout life expressing itself as infancy, childhood, adolescence, maturity, the decay and diseasing of senility and death.

What gains flow from the understanding?

The realization that man's diseases are largely an integral part of growth and development is an exercise in self-knowledge and self-respect. Such knowledge about ourselves, besides responding to the invocation to know ourselves can be preventive and curative for the current complex of diseasophobia and needless diagnosing and doctoring.

The acceptance of death as a timed event in a man's developmental programme governed by his herd, can mean divesting death of a thousand derogatory epithets. The current thanatological movement is pleading for giving death and the dying their due dignity. This is possible provided the modern, rational mind finds a place for disease and death in the logical scheme of things.

To understand disease and death is to accept them as parts of our own being. If life, as in its essence, is to be regarded as good, then death must be worshipped as life's guardian angel. Without death, none of us would be living as we are today. Let us understand life's foremost angel – death.

Such reverence for death has been, for long, epitomised in the Eastern concept of *Trimurti* (meaning, triple form). It is the Hindu triad of *Brahma* the Creator, *Vishnu* the Preserver, and *Shiva* the Dissolver. This holy trinity is represented carrying three confluent heads symbolizing the union of the three powers without whose blessings there can be no creation, nothing to preserve, and nothing to destroy.

The serene nonchalance and the effortless precision with which death exerts its sway at the appointed time *regardless* of any human expectations or efforts has earned for death the name of Dharmaraja/ Yamaraja* meaning Dutiful King/ Lawkeeping King. *Dharma* or *yama* or *niyama* in the Sanskrit language has the same connotation as *Tao*, meaning the Way of the primordial forces of nature, the mysterious laws that operate in

---

* Yamaraja is Yama the King. Yama with his twin sister and later his wife, *Yami* – both born of the rising sun Vivasvat and his consort Saranyu, the Goddess of clouds – formed the first couple to inhabit the earth. After their death, they have become the king and the queen of the realm of the dead where they have created and maintained dwellings of bliss for those who enter their kingdom. Yamaraja is the Supreme, kind ruler of the hereafter, the guarantor of bliss, and thus of Heavenly peace.

the great organic process of which man is but a part. Based upon the above and as an extension of it, any natural law or constant, or behavior (like gravity, or even the melting point of ice or iron) are assigned the appellation *yama, dharma,* or *niyama,* reminding one of the God of Einstein and Spinoza who reveals himself in the harmony of all beings, unconcerned with the fate and actions of individual man. All told, death is the *yama, niyama, dharma, tao,* and *nature* of one's being to be studied, treated and revered like any inherent force and aspect of nature.

CHAPTER 2   The Democracy of Disease

> Disease generally begins that equality which death completes.
>
> *Samuel Johnson*

An enquiry into the essential nature of human diseasing, provides an insight into the unswerving impartiality with which diseases treat mankind. The equality inherent in man's diseasing is a concept difficult to accept, but such difficulty need no longer allow man or medical science to deny its reality. The natural course of life exhibited by a human being, from conception to death, is similar the world over. Such similarity extends to that part of development called diseasing – be it heart attack or hypertension, cancer or diabetes. This Chapter is about the little but significant reading that we can make in the human body's unfathomable book of diseases.

What are diseases?

The number of diseases that makes up the medical lexicon is legion, but they can be broadly classified into two groups – *interactional* and *intrinsic*.

Interactional maladies arise as a consequence of the unfavourable interaction between a human being and his or her environment – nutritive (excess or deficiency), microbial (worms, bacteria, viruses), mechanical or allergic. All the interactional diseases lend themselves to control (antibiotics in infections) or prevention (no allergens, no allergy; no cars, no car-accidents; no tubercle bacilli, no tuberculosis). Modern medicine's golden-lettered triumphs have been in the field of interactional diseases – malnutrition mitigated, infections averted or treated, consequences of trauma minimized.

THE DEMOCRACY OF DISEASE

Intrinsic diseases, as the appellation implies, are coursal ("course" with "al" – not causal), programmed in one way or another into a human being's growth from the womb to the tomb, being the temporal signposts in the trajectory of an individual, and what is tellingly important, impervious to the march of modern medicine. The chief categories in this group are as follows:

Birth defects: These diseases are a result of the defective formation and/or functioning of some parts of the body, that an individual is born with. In medical parlance, these are called congenital malformations.

Metabolic or Constitutional disorders: These result from an alteration in the functioning of the body systems and comprise such diseases as diabetes, high blood pressure, high acid secretion in stomach, autoimmune diseases, and so on.

Tumor/Cancer: Some cells in the body change their character, and by multiplication form cell colonies, called a tumor or cancer.

Vascular diseases: With age, arteries throughout the length and breadth of the body harden, narrow, and even get blocked. When such a process affects the artery to the heart or to the brain, heart attack or stroke may result. In pathological terms, such vascular changes are also called arteriosclerosis or atherosclerosis.

Collagenous disorders: The cells and the blood vessels of the human body are supported by a universal network of fibers made up of the protein, collagen. The progressive changes in collagen fibers produce wrinkling of the skin, stiffening of the joints, and contribute to the diseasing of the arteries mentioned above.

Except for birth defects, all the other intrinsic disorders are an expression of the preprogrammed *ageing* of an individual.

DEATH

The problem of ageing

Ageing is the calendar of events that starts at conception, or more conventionally at birth, and ends only at death. Everything that lives *ages* with reference to a starting point in time. Ageing is synonymous with the passage of physical time, and need not be made to connote an adverse state or event.

Consistent with the ceaseless dynamism that characterizes life, an organism exhibits changes as it ages – changes that promote its survival, and almost *pari passu,* changes that demote its survival. At any stage, the individual's survival or otherwise is an outcome of the balance of these two sets of processes – the benescent ones and the senescent ones. A child that cuts its teeth so that it can bite better exhibits benescence; the same child if diagnosed to have diabetes or leukemia, exhibits senescence. A person aged 75, spontaneously recovering from an attack of pneumonia as a result of increased immunity against it, exhibits benescence. Senescence, then, is not restricted to the 'aged', nor is benescence a privilege only of the young; both can occur at any time from conception onwards. Ageing is a function of the calendar on the wall; benescing and senescing are functions of the changes exhibited by a growing organism.

These concepts and the concomitant insistence on clearer terminology, on ageing and senescence, have some illuminating implications:

1. Ageing is an extrinsic, physically-timed event; senescence comprises intrinsic bodily-timed tissue-changes. The two are related but not always. That is how time travels, in diverse paces with diverse persons, making the not-aged *look* senile, and the aged *look* young.

2. Senescence is co-extensive with the human lifespan. Etymologically, senescence is expected to occur only in a senile individual. Such a fixation must change. The criteria of senescence are *intrinsicality, progressiveness* and *deleteriousness.* A child of 4 years with, say, diabetes or cataract exhibits senescence, for each of these processes fulfills the above criteria.

The occurrence of diabetes as a disease with a wide age range – infancy to old age – during which it may manifest itself, should force us to revise our thinking on senescence. If diabetes or cataract in old age is looked upon as senescence consequent on ageing, why should the same in youth or even in infancy, be considered as anything but a form of senescence?

3. The signs of senescence can be altered to suggest that the changes brought about by ageing have been somehow reversed. Many a senescent process can be camouflaged, compensated for, even mitigated – grey hair dyed, lost teeth replaced by dentures, cataracts removed, wrinkles smoothed out by facelifts, baldness covered by a wig, and so on. However, the course of time cannot be diverted or altered.

At a more serious level, blocked arteries, of the heart or brain, can be cleansed, bypassed or replaced, cancerous masses removed, altered blood sugar curves restored to accepted norms, and so on. All these measures go a long way to ease the diseased, but fail to add to the individual's predetermined lifespan which is a function of ageing.

4. Much of medical prognosing (forecasting) on the course of a disease is judgment passed on mere appearances – an individual with altered EKG (ECG – Electrocardiogram), heightened sugar curves or blood pressure, or a cancer is given a 'bad' prognosis. On the other hand, a 'good' prognosis is given when a check-up reveals no abnormalities. On many an occasion, the prognosticator has been proved wrong: those given good prognosis die, those given poor prognosis, survive.

This medical predicament is rooted in the fact that diseased tissues and organs of the human body do not necessarily disease, get worse, or kill, nor are healthy-looking tissues and organs any guarantee against these possibilities.

Genesis of senescence and disease

A most popular suffix in modern medicine is *-gen* (from the Greek, *gennen* to produce). Its popularity springs from the idea that every disease – including senescence, and even death – has a cause. Hence the array of such specific terms as *atherogen, cancerogen, diabetogen, gerontogen* (or *senescogen*), *hypertensionogen,* and such general terms as *nosogen,* (from the Greek *nosos,* meaning disease) or *pathogen.* It is a sobering thought that much as such terms have given both credence and direction to medical thought and action, the end result, unfailingly, has proved the *nemesis* of the *-gen* concept, and with that, of the *-gen*-based research, prevention, and treatment. At the heart of Burnet's learned and devastating judgment against modern medicine – that the contribution of laboratory science to medicine has almost come to an end – lies the fact that as far as its *genocentric* (causalistic) approach to disease is concerned modern medicine has summarily failed.

Rudolf Virchow, the father of modern pathology, first proposed around 1858 the theory that a disease is the effect of some cause, which he has expounded in his book *Cellular Pathologie*. All diseases are asssumed to be the outcome of the 'changes' and 'active processes' that have taken place in the cells of the human body. From 1858 to 1984, medicine has vigorously searched for the *causal* changes in cells that breed diseases, and has failed completely. Of late, the thrust has not been so much on cells as on the molecules that make the cell – the new science of molecular biology. The outcome has been far from rewarding: the deeper insight into the nature of human diseasing, provided by such studies, has in fact underscored medical men's inherent inability either to elicit the causation of, or predictably and favourably alter the course of, say, cancer or heart attack, arthritis or autoimmune disease, stroke or senility. One is compelled to agree with Nobel-laureate Burnet's candor: 'I have more than once expressed the opinion that so far there has been no human benefit whatever from all that has been learnt of molecular biology. I doubt if any other biologist has been quite so blunt in public but a few eminent biochemists have agreed with me in private.' Summary failure on the molecular front has impelled the medical men to venture into the submolecular world – to no avail. The above assessment has a lesson – man is neither a molecule nor a mouse.

If the cells, and the submolecules and molecules that constitute them, have failed medical science, what of the substances that the cells themselves make, such as hormones? What of the loss of some vital hormones? The evidence so far does not support the idea that senescence is the result of decrease in the secretion of any single hormone, and castration in either sex appears neither to shorten life nor to alter the process of ageing.

While medical science has failed in its search for the specific causes of various maladies, its attempts to explain these on a general basis have not met with any success either. Gerontologists have been advancing the 'wear-and-tear' theory to explain senescence and diseases. While this theory is metaphorically most appealing, its mechanistic bias has failed to find any scientific evidence. Another general theory has it that the loss of reproductive fitness is tantamount to the loss of, in Darwin's terms, fitness to survive, thus resulting in diseases of old age. While the linking of reproductive capacity and the ability to survive may be acceptable at, say, the insect level, it finds poor application at the mammalian or human level.

In all humility, it must be concluded that medicine's search for a cause for many a disease that the human body is prone to has failed for want of any scientific support.

Why are there diseases?

The answer to the query 'Why are there diseases?' may be traced to the fact that man and animals are basically binary units comprising *cells* and the web or cocoon of *collagen fibers* that the cells throw around to house and support themselves. The cells and fibers together form such varied structures as skin, bone, liver, blood vessels, or intestines. Our cells and fibers, ever alive, ever changing, exhibit time-bound alterations that are at the heart of much of human diseasing. The study of the changes exhibited by cells and fibers could be called Cytofiber(ki)netics, or simply, cytofibernetics. It is not known whether the kinetics of cells and fibers are causally related or are merely concurrent.

DEATH

Our body cells have a *finite* capacity for replicating themselves. Admirably elegant studies on cells, employing their serial cultures in test tubes, have revealed animal cells to be endowed with species-specific doubling-capacity, proportional to the lifespan of the species. The cells from a human embryo can be made to double exponentially (in geometric progression) 45($\pm$5) times, whereas those from the rat embryo can be made to exhibit only 15($\pm$5) doublings. While the foregoing number, for human beings, appears miniscule *vis-a-vis* his lifespan of three score years and ten, its exponential nature makes it awesomely powerful. The entire human embryogenesis starting with one cell and ending up with many billions is an outcome of 32 exponential divisions.

What exact bearing does the finiteness of the doubling capacity of the animal cells have on the ageing and diseasing of the organisms is not understood. A cytologic feature is an indicator, however. As cells – having multiplied to meet with the normal demands of growing, living, and repair – approach the limit of their replicative capacity, they exhibit aberrations of chromosomes (gene-bearing bodies in cell nucleus) in number or structure, an *in vitro* (test tube) phenomenon probably occurring in the body as well. Cytologists and cancerologists tend to take chromosomal abnormalities as a prelude to, or accompaniment of, a cancerous change. Cancer, an eminently cellular phenomenon, underlies 20% of overall human diseasing.

Like cells, the collagen fibers senesce, the rate being species-specific, and inversely proportional to the lifespan of the species. Senescent collagen is degenerate collagen – drier, thicker, more rigid, shorter. Many of the ageing processes are apparently due to derangement in the structure of collagen. Skin wrinkles, joints stiffen, blood vessels thicken and harden. The coronary arteries disease to give heart attacks, the carotids (arteries of the brain) disease to give strokes, and the overall vascular diseases to give high blood pressure, and this totals up to over fifty per cent of human diseasing. There is considerable truth in the saying that a man is 'as old as his arteries'.

The balance is a group of human ailments that can neither be

THE DEMOCRACY OF DISEASE

clearly ascribed to the ageing of cells nor to the ageing of fibers – these are diabetes, a growing number of maladies called autoimmune diseases, and that ill-defined entity called loss of vitality or resistance. But there are pointers. Cells and fibers, on ageing and senescing, lose their pristine self-identity and pose as foreign elements that are attacked by the body's white cells much as these cells would attack invading microbes. The result is civil war, called autoimmune (immunity turned against one's self) diseases, that manifest themselves as diseases of joint, kidney, skin and so on. The aged white cells themselves may make the mistake of identifying the innocent self-units as foreign, unleashing an attack on them and breeding autoimmune diseases. The ageing white cells may also lose the ability to fight microbes, thus accounting for the loss of resistance in the aged.

It cannot be overemphasized that cytofibernetics and the ills that it breeds are no errors, no toll that we pay for the wear-and-tear of living, but a phyletic feature that cuts across the entire vertebrate kingdom, being an integral part of a genetically determined course that occurs independent of wear and tear. There are a thousand causalistic theories of ageing, senescing and (the consequent) diseasing, but each ends with the same refrain: *So far there is little evidence for this theory.* Ageing, senescence, disease and death are integral processes of biological maturation comprising a series of gradual changes that occur in the human body through time, from conception to death, as a part of the human life cycle.

Disease as a herd function

The term *herd* is synonymous with a group, community, population or an ethnic ensemble that, belonging to the same race and nationality, shares, what the geneticist calls, *a common or corporate gene pool* and through this, an interrelated pattern of diseasing, and death (See Chapter Three).

In any human community or herd, the *distribution* of cancer is in 1 out of every 5 persons. The occurrence of cancer in one person is thus a function shared by the other 4 who escape.

Considering further the distribution of, say, the age at which cancer occurs, it is found that amongst those who have cancer, the age-at-diagnosis is distributed along a bell-shaped curve, so that someone gets it at 19 years of age, the other at 91, the rest in between. Such *herd distribution*, and thus *herd control*, of a disease and its various features is found in all forms of human diseasing. A particular person's disease thus becomes an individual performance at the behest of the herd. The concept of *herd* (and *herdity*) highlights the interrelatedness of an individual and the rest of the group, whose corporate genetic programme determines the occurrence of disease, (and death) in the individual.

Democracy of diseases

Sir Thomas Browne, the English physician-philosopher, stated that the 'Mercy of God hath scattered the great heap of Diseases, and not loaded any one Country with all.' What Sir Thomas asserted in the seventeenth century continues to hold good in the twentieth. Barring interactional diseases – worm infestations occur because there are worms and skiing accidents occur because there are skiers – the intrinsic pattern is emerging as very impartial both in its occurrence and behaviour, be it the affluent West or the indigent East.

What distinguishes one country or a group from another – Alaska from Australia and India from Israel, American Negroes from American Whites – is not the total quantum of intrinsic diseases as much as their types. In a given population, birth defects – congenital malformations – affect a more or less fixed proportion of newborns, for these are an outcome of *multifactorial inheritance*, which is but the geneticists' way of saying that the occurrence of such abnormalities is a function of the herd and not of the individual affected nor of his or her parents. Cellular disease – cancer – occurs everywhere; in excess, nowhere. If the Parsi women in India have a greater incidence of breast cancer, the Hindus compensate for this difference by having a greater incidence of cervical cancer so that all told,

THE DEMOCRACY OF DISEASE

Parsis develop cancer and die with it no more nor less than their Hindu counterparts. Vascular diseases are universal and impartial. So is diabetes. To be human is to be endowed with one or more inherent, intrinsic diseases.

Stroke provides a striking example of the innate impartiality and universality of a disease. Stroke, medically called cerebrovascular disease, is a disease-complex arising from the disorder of the arteries supplying blood to the brain. A global epidemiological study on stroke revealed that at all ages it equally affects both sexes in all lands and all regions of the lands, being unrelated to environment, and not exhibiting any racial predeliction within a nation or between nations, regarding both its occurrence and behaviour. Such conclusions are equally relevant to other forms of human diseases. As the diseases caused by external factors – accidents, infections, malnutrition – are reduced, a greater number of human beings live out their natural lifespan. The longer they live, the more they exhibit diseases inherent to human ageing. This is universally true. Thus a curve describing mortality due to any intrinsic disease process closely compares with the age-specific mortality curve. The stroke mortality curve also describes such a pattern. If this is correct, then stroke may have to be classed as concomitant of ageing, and as such would seem to be preventable only to the extent that one could reverse the process of ageing.

If one were to replace in the foregoing, just the word 'stroke' by 'cancer', 'heart attack', 'hypertension', or 'diabetes', the generalization would hold as true. Each of the above diseases is built into mankind, into the warp and weft of man's genes. Being a herd feature that expresses itself at an individual level, a given disease affects a more or less fixed percentage of the herd, both as a herd certainty and an individual probability. All humans *can* develop, say, cancer or have a heart attack, yet only some *do*. It should not come as a surprise that carcinoma of the stomach, in the Japanese and Jamaicans, behaves in a very closely comparable fashion, despite the differing sophistry in medical care. So do heart attacks, hypertension and diabetes.

Human diseasing thus exerts its impartial sway on mankind

irrespective of such considerations as age, sex, heredity, race, religion, caste or creed, asceticism or hedonism, lowest Gross National Product or highest Gross National Product. The occurrence of heart attack, or stroke, carcinoma lung or carcinoma cervix, even in infancy, regardless of national boundaries bears an eloquent testimony to the democratic demeanour of diseases. On a global scale, paraphrasing Sir Thomas Browne, it could be reassuringly said that the mercy of God hath scattered diseases equally the world over, and hath commended them to behave comparably the world over. God has been very just.

CHAPTER 3   The Democracy of Death

> At the door stood Death. She said, 'I smelled your rooster and I came along to help you eat it.'
>
> 'And why not?' said the man. 'Aren't you one who treats everyone alike?'
>
> 'That is so,' said Death. 'I have no favorites. The poor, the rich, the young, the old, the sick, the well – all look alike to me.'
>
> 'That is the reason you may come in and share my food,' said the man. Death entered and the two had a grand feast.
>
> Aurora Lucero White-Lea

Death's inevitability is generally accepted; death's impartiality as expressed in the story quoted above, has remained in the realm of the incomprehensible. Death as a function of time and as the integral, climactic part of the normal, physiological development of man remains indifferent to the considerations of age, sex, nationality, Gross National Product, presence of disease, treatment or no treatment, good prognosis or bad. In death's democracy lies the explanation for the paradox of the diseased, the hedonistic and the devil-may-care outliving the healthy, the ascetic and the disciplined. The human body as a machine constantly acts counter to expectations; sometimes with every organ diseased, it still manages to drag along. This oddity lies neither in the human body nor in death, but in the erroneous assumptions of the lay, and more so, of the learned. A new 'Death View' – *Todesanschauung* – is in order: in the immutable democracy of death, all have equal rights, and all are treated impartially.

DEATH

Death is merciful – to man

The perceptible upswing in the graph of world population started around the beginning of the 15th century A.D. It has continued unabated, and today man has become the cancer of his own planet. The four billion *plus* human population of today will double itself in the next 33 years. Hasn't death been kind to man?

Today's man, under advice from modern medicine, fears death because of his much-voiced susceptibility to demonized diseases: heart attack, cancer, diabetes and so on, are all presented as all-consuming killers. Were these diseases as effectively lethal as paranoically portrayed, would man have turned into the cancer of the planet Earth? Isn't it that death's kindness is matched only by man's unkindness to man? In an age ruled by speed, terror and weapons, death by man-made violence stalks its quarry at every step, and since the year 1945, our species has acquired the diabolic power to annihilate itself. Isn't death then in the words of François Mauriac the 'one grace vouchsafed mankind'?

Death stands undisturbed

'Think of what has happened since 1950 . . . Progress in medicine has virtually eliminated many dread diseases. Most recent discoveries foretell the same fate for many others in the relatively near future.' This technological optimism expressed in an encyclopaedia is ill-founded. 'We might,' Comfort, the gerontologist, observes, 'in theory expect that removal of successive causes of death would increase the expectation of life of the old as well as the young. It is interesting to notice that there is so far very little evidence of such an effect from the general advances of medicine in the last century.' The presumed payoff from the inventions of immunization and antibiotics is being seriously doubted, the greater part (that is, ninety per cent) of the improvement in death rates from infections having already occurred prior to the introduction of immunization and antibiotics. In 1802, a committee of Scottish physicians wrote a memorandum declaring that the gains of medicine against breast cancer were a cipher; in the 1970s, other researchers reiterated the statement, adding that if at all, the mortality rate had increased. For example, at the Johns Hopkins Hospital, the impact of radionuclide scanning for brain tumors was assessed from 1962 to 1972. The number of brain scans increased ten-fold in that decade, and for patients with tumors the average interval between the onset of symptoms and operation fell from four years to less than one. Yet there was no favourable change in survival after operation.

The widely acclaimed increase in human life-expectancy, the world over, is an outcome of some unflattering phenomena. Semmelweis, Lister and good obstetrics meant more babies survived, thus widening the base of the human population pyramid, the widening effect seen throughout, from base to apex. Now, more people live into old age just because there are more people. This demographic upsurge long presaged medical advances which, however, took the credit as these advances arrived *pari passu* with a peak in the exponentially expanding human population. Death *per se*, however, has serenely defied the march of modern medicine.

Death prevails, because, as Tagore says, *Death belongs to life as birth does.* Balancing the 'will-to-live' natural to every organism there is the 'will-to-leave.' Each human being, as an animal, is born with a built-in death wish, or death programme together with an intrinsic mechanism for fulfilling the same, somewhere in his or her body. The will-to-leave, may reside in the brain cells of an Isaacs, the discoverer of interferon, in the pancreas of a Dr. Knowles, lately the President of the Rockefeller Foundation, or in the blood vessels of a Nietzsche, a Nehru, or a Brezhnev.

'The aim of all life is death' – with this aphorism, Freud formulated, in 1920, his concept of a death instinct or death wish. According to Konrad Lorenz, Freud's theory of the death wish is a destructive principle which exists as an antithesis to all instincts of self-preservation, and is therefore both unnecessary and false.

It must be made clear that the will-to-leave, as proposed above, has a fundamental protoplasmic or cellular quality that is independent of the Freudian psyche or the Lorenzian lore. It simply is, wherever life is, served by a built-in death programme.

Death: A herd function

Death, like disease, is a herd function. It treats a given human herd in 3 distinct, sequential phases – *herd trimming, herd stability,* and *herd lysis.* Herd trimming ensures herd quality control to eliminate the defective concepti, fetuses and newborns. Herd trimming starts from the stage of conception, whence it is at its peak, and in a diminuendo fashion, operates till about the age of five years. This explains 'fetal wastage' in the form of spontaneous, unpreventable abortions, infant mortality which is the highest in the first day of life, leukemia having its most lethal effect in the first year of life whatever the treatment, the greater incidence of cancer in the first five years of life than during either of the two ensuing quinquennia, and the rather fixed incidence of major birth defects. This may seem a wasteful and cruel method, but no living species can escape this relentless force of natural selection. The same acausal and uncontrollable factors as govern diseases and death in the adult human subserve herd trimming. Herd trimming paves the way for the phase of herd stability.

During the phase of herd stability, disease and death are at their lowest ebb, well-nigh close to the baseline. No wonder that the incidence of and the mortality from cancer, for example, reaches an all-time low. Starting at 6 and extending up to about the age of 16, this most generous phase of human survival allows 97% of the herd who escaped herd trimming to reach the state of reproductive fitness. And then starts the gradual, but relentless crescendo phase of herd lysis.

The phase of herd lysis may be defined as the Age-Dependent Obligatory Herd Mortality that begins around the age of 15-16, very low in intensity to start with, and doubling every 8 years. Graunt in 1662 and Gompertz in 1825, both from England, were the pioneers in the presentation and prediction of such programmed herd mortality, often known as the Gompertz function which cuts across all species barriers – e.g., the mortality in rats, closely parallel, *mutatis mutandis*, to that in man, doubles every 30 days. The gentle beginnings of herd lysis allow most people to get into their forties, whereafter only the lethal impact of Gompertz function starts being felt. Gompertz function is an integral group function that is remarkably impartial, and highly democratic. Its inexorable sway explains the failure of modern medicine to add even one year to the human life span. The Vedic blessing of 100 years and the Biblical blessing of three score and ten are no modern inventions.

The increase in vulnerability with age is an all-round and non-specific process. For example, even the age distribution of pedestrian deaths in road accidents is similar in contour to the general distribution of human deaths from all causes. This is but an illuminating reflection of herd vigour, in its biological sense, for it represents a combination of sensory acuity, speed of avoidance, and power of recovery when hit. Needless to say, the function of herd mortality is not cause-crazy. It achieves a common end through seemingly diverse diseases. One would never have thought of any similarity among chronic lymphatic leukemia, disseminated breast cancer, cirrhosis of liver, and heart attack. But the similarity is very close in the way each disease takes its toll of mankind. The epidemiologists, who detected the similarity, found it surprising that the above diseases resembled each other very closely in the relationship between their mortality rate and the duration of disease. Furthermore, the nature of this relationship in all these diseases was quite unexpected: the basic death rate remained constant during the entire course of the disease. Prognosis was neither better nor worse for the patient late in the disease than for the patient early in the disease; the patients neither 'got over' the disease nor did they develop cumulative damage that progressively increased their death rate. And the similarity was unaffected even when a variety of standard treatments or no treatment at all was employed for the different diseases. This also meant that even within a single group, say of chronic lymphatic leukemia, treatment made no difference to the overall survival or mortality.

DEATH

Memento mori: Death here and now

> And had you watched Ahab's face that night, you would have thought that in him also two different things were warring. While his one live leg made lively echoes along the deck, every stroke of his dead limb sounded like a coffin-tap. On life and death this old man walked.
>
> *Herman Melville*

All of us, newborn to nonagenarians, walk on life and death. The common lament that the young never consider the prospect of their death is rooted in death's mild, almost imperceptible sway on this side of 40. Yet no year of human lifespan is exempt from death, *here and now*. Mortality tables on heart attack, stroke, cancer and infections bear a telling testimony to the above. That the young are not used to thinking of the hour of their death is trite; it is this *habit* carried into old age that underlies many human problems.

Time: Death's sole weapon

Given any of the so-called killer diseases – heart attack, cancer, diabetes, etc. – modern medicine has been unable to say which patient would die from the disease, and when. Take the example of acute heart attack: the outcome of a heart attack, in a given person is unpredictable. On the one hand, this is because of the constant threat of sudden unexpected death, even for persons convalescing favourably, and on the other hand because of the possibility of *long survival even for persons critically ill.* In November 1972, Dr. B, aged 58 years, a leading physician and cardiologist in Bombay, went to see a heart patient in an Intensive Coronary Care Unit (ICCU); Dr. B developed chest pains while seeing the patient, and died soon after, in the ICCU.

Notwithstanding the absence of a correlation between the severity of a disease and death, what has been predictably observed is the unswerving nature of age-dependent herd mortality that obeys the age of a human herd. And as yet, the only infallible way to measure a herd's age is time. Time, then, is the sole weapon that death wields, with severe disregard for doctors' diagnoses and prognoses. For each one of us, 'the end is at hand' and 'the measure full,' when 'our time is up' – at the herd level always a certainty: at the individual level, a blissfully unpredictable probability.

The cause of death: So-called

The realization that time is the only ally death has, drives home that the cause of death, a long-cherished medical, epidemiological or public institution, is an *a posteriori* assessment in all natural (non-accidental) deaths, a situation that allows us to paraphrase Pascal: death has its own reasons which are quite unknown to the doctor.

One of the 'more popular' teaching-exercises in medical schools is the clinicopathological conference, where the gross and microscopic postmortem findings are correlated *a posteriori* with the clinical features so as to arrive at *the* diagnosis and *the* cause of death. Over the years, such conferences have been a theater for defensive gamesmanship, display of pedantic erudition and, despite all these intellectual acrobatics, they have served no epistemological purpose in medicine. No wonder such retrospective exercises are now held as obsolete by discriminating thinkers in medicine.

Consider some typical obituary announcements for both sexes: Death from heart attack at 48, 61, 77, 81, from cancer at 40, 42, 69 and no cause – old age? – at 88 and 108. Why fatal heart attack at 48 at one end and 81 at the other, giving the fallacious but favourite average age of fatal heart attack as 65? What turns out more influential, the age or the attack? Take cancer: if cancer itself does not kill by and large, and if treatment reputedly prepones death, what or who was responsible for death in lung cancer cases, one at 42, the other at 69? The American hotel magnate Conrad Hilton died of pneumonia at 91. Why did Mr.

Hilton not get the same pneumonia at 89? And what if he had not had the pneumonia? It is a general autopsic observation that people dying in advanced age show their bodies to be a veritable museum of various pathologies, each as terminal and as lethal as the other. Usually one amongst these emerges – or so it is assumed, to be labelled as *the* cause of death. Hence the question remains as to what was more important – the host of pathologies that Mr. Hilton must have had for decades, or the fact that he was 91? Death, the climax of an inner developmental process, occurs when the timer from within rings to say that 'the time is up'. Diseases are pointers to the proximity of death, not causal; and isn't life the most incurable disease?

The democracy of death

Death has been called the great leveller. The appellation need be no different when it is probable death, for it fully satisfies Mahatma Gandhi's idea of a democracy in which the weakest enjoy the same opportunities as the strongest.

In an age steeped in the Darwinian concept of survival of the fittest, Gandhi's invocation appears impracticable, out of place. That isn't so. As Arthur Koestler pointed out in his book *Janus: A Summing Up*, 'Once upon a time, it all looked so simple. Nature rewarded the fit with the carrot of survival and punished the unfit with the stick of extinction. The trouble only started when it came to defining "fitness" . . . What exactly are the criteria of "fitness"? The first answer that comes to mind is: the fittest are obviously those who survive the longest.' Those who survive the longest may have satisfied neither the Darwinian decree of reproductive fitness nor the medical criteria of physical fitness. Death, in its impeccable impartiality, is above all this.

Death does not spare the young; the old do outlive them. When in a memoir to his son, who in his teens died of a brain tumor, John Gunther cried *'Death Be Not Proud,'* he could as well have said, *'Death Be Not So Damned Just.'* In *The Rape of Lucretia,* Lucretia's father cries: 'If children predecease progenitors, we are their offsprings, and they none of ours.' The fact

THE DEMOCRACY OF DEATH

that not many parents have to lament like Lucretia's father, does not mean that death fails to be democratic. It is just that its mathematics work in a lower key at a younger age, in animals and men.

As to gender, death is democratic, with a slight difference – women live longer than men, a fact that forms an outstanding contradiction to the Darwinian dogma of reproductive fitness as necessary for survival: the human female happens to be the only mammal divested of her reproductive function when she is hardly half-way through her natural lifespan. Darwinism has fostered the concept of the survival of the fittest rated according to the ability to reproduce. If we were therefore to believe that the loss of the ability to reproduce is tantamount to the loss of the capacity to survive, we cannot but conclude that menopause, inevitable as it is in every human female by about the age of 45-47 years, is not merely a change of life but the loss of life-sustaining selection pressure. On the other hand, although function of the testes does tend to decline slowly with advancing age, the evidence is clear that there is no male menopause or climacteric similar to that occurring in women. Naturally, the perennially potent and fertile man, ever ready to contribute 'to the gene pool of the succeeding generation', should possess an outright and consistent advantage in survival capacity over the human female. But, alas, in reality exactly the opposite prevails. From birth onwards, in every age group life is shorter for males than for females, the death rates for males consistently exceeding those for females in the average ratio of about 1:5:1 for all age groups.

This has been the case over the centuries the world over. However, death's favour to the fair sex ends at that. The mathematics of *herd trimming* and *herd lysis* in the female operate in the same way as in the male. The curves of mortality in both the sexes remain closely parallel and the incidence of cancer and of stroke remains equal. Prior to menopause, coronary artery disease affects women less; but thereafter, almost in a hurry, it catches up with the incidence in men, so that the end result – that is, the number of heart attacks per 100 deaths – comes out to be the same in both the sexes.

DEATH

Now some factors remain – presence of disease, administration of treatment, or when a doctor himself is the patient – that bear testimony to death's democracy. The affliction of a major disease is no bar to living long. Louis Pasteur had a nearly lethal stroke at 47, and lived most creatively till the age of 74. A man found to have Hodgkin's disease at the age of 29 developed 11 different cancers, one after another, during the next 27 years. One Mrs. R., known personally to the authors, lived to be a vigorous 99, having nursed an untreated bladder cancer for her last 32 years. The treated exhibit no survival advantage over the non-treated, even in the medically most advanced countries, where sophistication borders on the Utopian. In a study by Cregan and others, of the 150 patients treated with Paulingian megadoses of vitamin C, the only long-term survivor for 63 weeks and more against the average 7 weeks was a patient with massive liver-jaundice, and a widespread cancer that had refused to show any response to many attempts at chemotherapy; and as a 'control' this very case had been denied vitamin C. Doctors are no exception to death's democracy. Bernard Shaw preached this through *The Doctor's Dilemma:* 'Make it compulsory for a doctor using a brass plate to have inscribed on it, in addition to the letters indicating his qualifications, the words "Remember that I too am mortal."' The Koran implores medical men to treat the diseased, and the dying, with extreme humility – a gentle, inner submission that 'It could have been me.'

Democracy of dying

Death, devoid of its presumed dependence on a disease for achieving its aim, assumes the role of a physiological process. The innate wisdom of the human body sees to it that the climactic event of death actuates physiological mechanisms that facilitate the function of giving up one's mortal frame. The discovery of encephalin, recently honoured with a Nobel prize, the body's own morphine, a potent, ever ready antidote to any pain, points to the possibility that there are other substances, indigenous to our body and released at the time of death, that smooth the

THE DEMOCRACY OF DEATH

passage through the door of death.

The common fear that dying is a painful process fails to be vindicated by what is known about dying. There is no denying that certain illnesses are painful, but death itself tends not only to be not painful, but also brings relief from pain. All competent observers agree that except in the imagination, there is no such thing as death agony. In fact, if one were to summarize the recent reliable reports from persons who, once declared dead came back, it would be – 'Death is the final delight.'

Death, delightful and friendly; but for whom? And how? For us, all of us provided we have realized well in advance the inevitablity of the final moment and its impartial luminescence. What has hitherto been considered apocryphal, or at best anecdotal, has been shown to be a fairly common, illuminating death experience, bordering on the divine or the supernatural. Regardless of the age, sex, past illness, past deeds, learnedness or otherwise, the act of dying bestows on an individual beatific blissful experience, devoid of any sense of fear, with unseen loving guides close enough not to allow the dying person to feel lonely. Before breathing their last, dying persons move away from their corporeal self to serve as witness – autoscopy – to the event. Dying persons who returned to life 'from the embrace of eternity' stress the need in this life of cultivating love for others as *the* prime necessity of existence.

If we are wonderfully made, and as wonderfully maintained, is there less reason to assume that the same spirit sitting within us sees to it that we are no less wonderfully unmade! If the sheer beauty and complexity of ontogeny (formation of one's self) is everybody's privilege, the same must hold true for the glory and the grandeur of ontolysis (dissolution of one's self) – the climactic moment of merger with the infinite.

CHAPTER 4   Death: Design and Definition

> Dost thou ask some boon, O Kunti's Son,
> I will grant it.
> Except immortality alone, tell me
> as to the desire that is in thy heart.
>
> Lord Krishna to Arjuna
In The Mahabharata, Vana Parva

'Ask, and it shall be given,' – having said so, the Lord hastens to add 'except immortality alone', for to so ask and so grant would be against the nature of things. The Mahabharatian mandate has survived the passage of 2,500 years and the marvels of modern medicine.

In one way or another, the scriptures have striven to drive home this lesson of death's inevitability, and indispensability. Lord Buddha's way of consoling the mother who lost her only son was to ask her to go into the town and bring him 'a little mustard seed from any house where no man hath yet died.' Achilles, the greatest and the ablest Greek hero, was left with a vulnerable heel; Duryodhan, the Kaurava prince in the *Mahabharata,* was blessed with head-to-foot invulnerability, save an area on the upper thigh. Lord Krishna himself was fatally wounded by a hunter's arrow piercing his foot. A patient survived a heart transplant to die of stomach cancer.

A Bengali proverb puts it rather tartly: When the snake has bitten on the head, where should one tie the tourniquet? The understanding of death as an integral design within us is to accord to death the long-denied status of a physiological process. It is to discover the Achilles heel in Everyman.

Death: life's invention

Robert Ardrey, the noted anthropologist, has described death as life's most startling invention. Before a certain moment in the history of living things, Ardrey observes, death did not exist. And then, it arrived on the biological stage, as an invention of life to give meaning to life.

Jacob, the French biologist and Nobel prize winner, ends his classic *The Logic of Living Systems* with a generalization that but for death, evolution could not have been: 'Not death from without, as the result of some accident; but death imposed from within, as a necessity prescribed from the egg onward by the genetic programme itself.'

This essay on evolution argues that the forces of life have fashioned the forces of death, making death integral to life, as physiologically mediated as life, and in terms of the individual's growth and maturation, a designed denouement that climaxes a series of timed events. It is significant that death as a function has been found to be independent of the presence or the absence of disease.

Death as a physiological process

The science of physiology (from *physiké* = the science of nature) has been defined as 'the philosophy of function in living matter, encompassed in this philosophy being the study of factors responsible for the origin, development and progression of life.' In this definition, the bias towards living and life is clear; no wonder death as a subject does not enjoy a place in physiology texts, and an authoritative medical encyclopaedia accords it no mention at all. It needs to be realized that living and dying, and life and death are but the two sides of the same coin, what the Zen scholar Alan Watts calls, *The Two Hands of God*.

Living is dying

Granted that living starts at conception, so does the countdown in the organism's march towards the ultimate event of death.

DEATH

Science's acceptance that the scriptural idea of the finite number of heartbeats or breaths that a person or an animal is allotted in his or her lifetime may be right, reveals as a direct consequence that a heartbeat or a single act of breathing, while demonstrating the process of living is at the same time an act irretrievably lost towards the process of dying.

Should there be an insistence that dying is equivalent only to diseasing, let it be realized that, integral to man's biological trajectory, diabetes actually begins at conception, vascular disease – 'a song that is first sung in the cradle', responsible for heart attack, stroke or kidney failure – begins in childhood, and a cancer occurring at the age of 56 is a part of the individual's programme from the very beginning. The sophisticated medical check-ups that lay claims to early diagnoses are examples of ill-founded medical optimism. The infinite mercy of the process of dying rests in its discreet silence. All of us die *with* far more diseases than we die *of*, and all these including the presumably lethal diseases, remain discreetly silent for almost the whole lifespan.

Cellular bases of disease and death

The nearly 6000 billion cells that comprise a human being may be broadly classified into two groups: the short-lived dividing cells, and the perennial or immortal non-dividing cells. To the former group belong the blood cells, blood vessel cells, skin cells, kidney cells and so on, which together form the *supporting complex* mediating the respiratory, circulatory, nutritive, excretory and reproductive functions. The 'immortal' group *perennial complex* comprises the sensory receptors, nerve cells and the muscle cells which in concert constitute the *essence* of an individual, being the seat of his affective, cognitive, and conative faculties.

Human life starts as a single cell, the zygote formed by the union of the sperm and the ovum. By dint of very rapid cellular multiplication accompanied by the mysterious process of cell differentiation, the zygote transforms itself into a fully formed human being by the end of the 8th week after conception.

DEATH: DESIGN AND DEFINITION

Thereafter, throughout the fetal life and the total adult life span, the cells of the supporting complex and those of the perennial complex behave as polar opposites.

The cells of the supporting complex are small cells – a typical mammalian cell measures about 10 microns in diameter. This complex increases its bulk by cell multiplication. Some of the types of cells falling into this category continue to multiply at rates faster than the fastest growing cancer. Yet, the cell number remains constant everywhere by a corresponding rate of elimination of the cells by surface loss or destruction. The faculty of cellular multiplication enables the supporting complex to regenerate, repair, migrate from one site to another like blood cells, and be grafted by the surgeon from one site to another as in transplantation. The ability of the cells to multiply is the most outstanding feature of the supporting complex.

The inability of the cells to multiply beyond the 8th week of life in the womb, is the cardinal feature of the perennial complex. Its constituent cells are formed – in trillions – once and for ever, aligned to each other by very precise, point-to-point connections.

The cells of the perennial complex are incapable of regeneration, i.e. replacement of damaged cells or those lost due to disease or injury. The perennial complex increases its size to keep pace with the growth of the individual not by an increase in cell number (unlike the supporting complex) but by an increase in cell size. In a man 6 feet in height, some of the nerve cells are 6 feet 6 inches long, and some of the muscle cells are over a foot in length. The whole complex is an incredible computer with infinite intercellular connections. Because the cells of this complex do not divide, the connections are not disturbed and hence the precision and accuracy of this computer are assured throughout life.

The supporting complex is our Achilles heel, for senescence and for death, being the target area for the 10,000 shocks that flesh is heir to. The ability of the cells of the supporting complex to divide *normally* makes them prone to divide *abnormally* to form tumors, benign or malignant. The cells of the perennial complex cannot divide normally or abnormally. The tumors of the brain and the spinal cord arise from the neuroglial cells, a part of the supporting complex. There are as many as ten neuroglial cells providing support and nutrition to one nerve cell. The cells of the supporting complex, because of their multiplicability, are highly sensitive to damage and death by radiation whereas the cells of the perennial complex by their freedom from multiplicability, are immune to radiation damage.

The collagenous network and the intercellular 'cement' that form the general matrix for cells and organs, make integral part of the supporting complex and senesce at parallel rates. This means that there is much more to the frailty and fragility of the supporting complex than we suspect. Its universal network of blood vessels is prone to thickening, stiffening, encrustation and occlusion. (Some researchers hold that the so-called atheromatous process, or atherosclerosis, is a variant of tumor formation from multiplication of cells lining the blood vessels). The blockage of an artery from the heart spells heart attack, of the brain – stroke, of the kidney – high blood pressure and kidney failure, of the limbs or intestine – gangrene. It is not the heart that primarily fails or infarcts, for its muscle cells belong to the immortal perennial complex. In fact, the heart's blood vessels – the coronaries – are the ones that let it down. The coronary arteries form the recipient part of our Achilles heel, an area that the death-arrow strikes conclusively.

The other sundry maladies – graying of hair, loss of teeth, wrinkling of skin, diabetes, arthritis, metabolic disorders, diseases of immunity – are all in the realm of the supporting complex. The perennial complex is largely exempt even from the ubiquitous microbial infections. Nature in its infinite wisdom has so designed us that ageing, senescence and disease leave our better self – our mind, our brain, our senses – essentially unmolested so that Pablo Picasso could creatively paint in his 80's, and Voltaire could write *Irene* late in life. Above all, for these exceptional and for us ordinary mortals, the continuing vigor of the perennial complex allows us to feel the bliss of being, perceive the mercy of God, have possibly the most sublime *mental composure* in the hour of our death, and to welcome death, like Rabindranath Tagore or St. Francis of Assisi, with arms wide open.

What is true of man is true of all vertebrates. Animals too have a perennial complex that is immortal, and a supporting complex that by its programmed fragility, its timed mortality, determines the lifespan of the species in general and of an animal in particular. Beyond the differences in the time-scale, diseases in animals bear a striking similarity to diseases in man, be it diseased coronaries or a cancerous stomach. The cancer of the breast, or of the blood in a dog, or Hodgkins's disease in a pig, can be passed off as corresponding cancer of a human being if the identity of the source is not revealed.

Disease doesn't cause death

The formidable array of pathological processes to which one's supporting complex is prey fails to help medical men to comprehend the genesis of death. Diseased, very diseased, persons survive; healthy, 'too good to die' persons collapse and die. A person with manifest disease of the coronary arteries outlives his fellow with 'normal' arteries; a treated or excised cancer fails to guarantee survival; the presence of untreated cancer, even advanced cancer, fails to guarantee death. Diseasing is the time-bound temperament of our tissues; death is a timed event that is largely independent of the nature or the extent of the disease process.

Over the past 200 years, from the time that the autopsy (the postmortem) became routine practice, medicine has tried to study diseases to understand the genesis of death, but has failed. Medicine's pathological approach assumes that the presence of pathology must lead to disease on the one hand, and death on the other. On both counts, medicine has been proved wrong. Most pathological processes remain discreetly silent and as experience shows, beg to be left untouched. The idea that death is caused by a particular disease or diseases has proved so unreliable that an American researcher-writer, Mack Lipkin, in *The New England Journal of Medicine* has rightly described the charade of an autopsy and the related clinicopathologic conference, as anachronistic.

What kind of death for whom?

To cite but one example, let us consider the occurrence of death in a cancer patient. The patient has advanced cancer, and the patient, physician, and the next of kin are virtually waiting for the cancerous axe to snap the cord of the patient's life. But cancer fails, for heart attack or stroke overtakes and beats cancer to the final post. Patients do not necessarily die of the disease from which they have suffered for so long. To the question concerning what kind of death for what kind of patient, the most scientific reply would be to express admission of medical ignorance. The lay and the learned are interested in knowing how death would come, and which disease would cause it. One can be wiser only after the event.

Defining death

While at death, we may define it. A clear definition of death (until recently, no great problem) has now become a pressing need, in academia, hospitals and courts, because of the emergence of organ transplantation. The transplant surgeon is plagued by a clinical paradox with regard to the organ-donor: he or she should give a live functioning organ from a live, active body although such a donor, to be a donor, should be assumed dead. The transplant paradox has been resolved by the invention of the concept of brain-death, 'which declares a person dead when the brain is not functioning even though the heart beats on.'

This intellectual compromise, the definition of convenience labelled 'brain-death', is made in the face of the facts that (a) except for the surface areas of the cerebral hemispheres, the rest of the brain is neither inactive nor dead; (b) the major systems of circulation, respiration, digestion, excretion and even reproduction are alive and actively functioning, and (c) because of (b), all the *vital signs* are present. The unmistakable imprints of individuality – the physiognomy, the finger prints, the immune system actively opposed to any foreign protein in the form of microbes or a graft – are all untouched in brain-death. Death as we have known it, aims at disincarnation, a dissolution of the body by enzymatic and microbial forces released from within the body. No such thing happens after brain-death. No wonder it has been alleged that, in the absence of an unquestionable definition of death in the world of transplantation, the overweening enthusiasm of the transplant surgeon has meant assuming that organ-donors are dead when they are far from being so.

A way of defining death is to define life; from the womb to the tomb. The human body is an assemblage of different, highly specialized systems that are reciprocally connected to one another and to the external world by the universal network of blood vessels that derive their life-giving throb from a vigorous central pump called the heart. Even the nascent human embryo, which starts as an amorphous mass of cells in no way recognizable then as a human form, presages this need: the very first functioning system it fashions is the heart and its blood vessels that are present by the 4th week after fertilization, at a time when *no* other system is anywhere around. Students of the chick embryo can see, by the forty-fourth hour of the development of a chick, the tiny, bright, red heart with its blood vessels as the island throbbing with life in the otherwise absolutely featureless egg. The cell-to-cell universality of the circulatory system – heart and blood vessels – provides it with the pristine primacy of enlivening and interconnecting all other systems, giving each of them a meaning, a purpose, be it in a fully healthy individual, a deeply comatose patient, or a crusader fasting to death. We can generalize that the heartbeat – as felt over the heart or the peripheral pulse – representing active circulation of blood is the lowest common, debate-free denominator of life. The heartbeat is life. Its absence is death. Human life, in a manner of speaking, is a brief spell of existence between two heartbeats, man's first and man's last.

The unrestricted, unconditional and universal applicability of the above definition of life and death based on the presence or absence of a functioning circulatory system may be realized from the fact that (a) the anesthetists who take humans into a deep, reversible coma must *keep* the circulatory system going, (b) the cardiac surgeons who, during surgery, put the heart and/or lungs out of action must *maintain* the circulatory system by machines, and (c) the resuscitators who bring back to life a person who has had a cardiac arrest or has been buried and frozen in snow, must, above all, *revive* the circulatory system. If blood is circulating, life is. If not, death is. Needless to say, the above definition of and approach to the ascertainment of life or death is applicable with ease by everyone, everywhere.

Brain-dead people are heart-alive, and therefore not dead. The solution to the current acrimonious debate about brain-death is the medical candor that sees a live individual as live, and not as dead just because a part of the brain is not functioning. Such an unconscious patient is a live donor, like any other live donor, and should be respected and treated as such.

Why death is, the moment the heartbeat is not?

Broadly speaking, a human being is comprised of the circulatory, respiratory, nervous, digestive, excretory, reproductive, and locomotor systems. All these systems – each a highly evolved biologic unit – are knitted into an organic whole by the prime unit of heart and blood vessels. Two features of each of these systems – structural and functional reserve on the one hand, and summary dispensability on the other – merit discussion here.

Each one of us has been provided by a generous, almost profligate Nature with a lot of extra liver, extra kidney substance, extra endocrines, extra lungs, extra brain and so on. Even the vulnerable heart and its vulnerable blood vessels are endowed with a surprising structural and functional reserve (The pairing of most of the organs is the body's survival instinct in action). Hence, although each system decays and diseases with age, life, good active life, goes on. With advancing age, the functional demands on each system decline, so that a degenerate or diseased organ still continues to be compatible with good living. The heart, too, takes a good deal of punishment before giving up. There are persons who get a series of heart attacks over a period of many years and pull through every time to lead to a long life. Even a heart attack, *per se* is not the cause of death. Hence, in fact, the surprising but certain dissociation between the presence of disease and the occurrence of death.

Experimental physiology and clinical experience have shown that life can continue, even unaided, in the absence of lung function for a few heart beats, in the absence of the liver for a few days, of the gut or the kidneys for a few weeks, of the endocrines for a few months, of the brain – brain-death – for a few years, of the limbs (as in thalidomide children) for a lifetime. The only indispensable unit is the heart and its blood vessels. Without them life ceases to be, even though all other systems may be in perfect condition. When death does occur in states of liver, kidney or endocrine disorders, the final decisive point is the cessation of the heartbeat. Heartbeat, present or absent, is thus the final arbiter of the presence or absence of life.

The question of sudden death

The realization that the cessation of heartbeat is the only incontrovertible element in the genesis and diagnosis of death bears relevance to the problem of sudden death.

Consider the deaths of Mahatma Gandhi felled by an assassin's bullets, of King George the VI who died in his sleep, of Jawaharlal Nehru long-ailing from a stroke, of Gamal Abdul Nasser long-ailing from diabetes, and of you and me, one in the best of health, dying on the spot from the very first heart attack and the other dying after a series of heart attacks or after a protracted illness of the liver/kidneys/brain etc. When did death occur? Was it sudden or gradual?

Death, in health or in illness, either without any injury or following injury, is always a *sudden* event, being but the small decisive gap between the presence of heartbeat and the permanent, total absence of the immediate next beat. Bullets tore through Gandhi's heart, yet he *lived* for a brief while, and in utter grace, said 'Hey Rama.' From the time the bullets were pumped in, to the time his heart beat its last, he was alive, only to die *suddenly* when the next heart beat did not come. The same for the King of England, for Nehru, for Nasser, for someone in absolute health, and someone in extreme illness.

What people actually mean by 'sudden death' is unexpected death, both in health and in sickness. This attitude of not expecting death stems from lay and learned ignorance of the constant proximity of death during any phase of life, and the obsession that only the presence of advanced illness is the harbinger of death. On both counts people and physicians have been proved wrong. The sudden death of a person in good health is a climactic event that the person's body was preparing for without the knowledge and permission of his or her doctors. On the contrary, when the doctors give up a case as hopeless and as facing imminent death, the body declares that, for individual and herd reasons, its time has not yet ended, and in the teeth of medical opinion, continues to live. The medical arrogance and its misplaced confidence in its 'objective' tests is best shown in a cartoon that appeared in the *Science Digest* 1979. It shows a physician rather overbearingly declaring to the distraught patient seated across the table: 'Of course, we'll have to wait for the lab tests, but according to our diagnostic computer – you're dead!'

CHAPTER 5   The Trans-Science Aspects of Disease and Death

> The big brag preceded the big bang as a human possibilty. Any demonstration that the earth revolves about the sun, while offensive to the authorities in charge, did not presume that we could reverse its course. Any proof of a natural law called gravity did not presuppose that man could make apples fall up; designers of supersonic planes, indeed, still take account of the apple. To the frontiersmen of science the discovery of natural laws meant no more than that we had explored certain forces governing the dispositions of man. But for many a hoi-polloi scientific settler who came after the frontier such discoveries meant something quite different: Man could master nature.
>
> Robert Ardrey

The cardinal psychological prerequisite for accepting diseases, death and their democracy is the realization that the denial of these lies in the realm of the impossible. The task before us is to discover certain natural forces and laws governing the nosologic (*noso* = disease) and the thanatologic dispositions of man. And such discovery reveals to us the trans-scientific nature of human disease and death.

A word about trans-science: Weinberg, introducing this concept and term, defines 'trans-science' questions as those that can be asked *of* science, but cannot be answered *by* science. Epistemologically, these are questions of facts presentable in the language of science but to which science has no rational answers; such questions transcend science. For example, about the 'why?' of the invariable variability of a person, from birth through death, questions have been asked of medical science, but have not been answered by medical science. Modern medicine, in its ostensibly scientific optimism, has not accorded due consideration to factors that are not only trans-modern-medicine but trans-*any*-science.

At the root of medicine's failure in providing an answer to the questions of what, when, how, where and who is an assemblage of four independent biological factors; *time, uncertainty, relativity,* and *normality*. These abstract principles govern all that appears concrete in medicine be it laboratory research or the development of a person, physiological parameters, disease, and death. Such an approach is both an analysis and a synthesis, discussed in the order of time, relativity, normality, uncertainty, and the overall implications thereof.

Time

Time is as fundamental as space and holds perhaps the essence of all reality. If matter has been understood as but configured energy, then life needs to be understood as configured time. Isn't man, from his very start as a zygote, a calendar of timed events? Human development, in the mother's womb, is charted with remarkable precision in terms of weeks, days, and hours.

Lest the proposition that every life-form represents a unique, individualized space-time entity appear preposterous, it is pertinent to allude to Einstein's concept that regards *matter* as the expression of an inner dynamic *will* that is natural, meaningful or even divine. If matter can be assigned such individualized qualities as 'will' and 'inner essence', there should be no objection to assigning each individualized life-form the status of a unique space-time unit. In a symposium titled *Man and Time,* Portmann characterizes any life-form as configured time, while Van der Leeuw pithily concludes: 'We *are* time'. Burnet relates time to disease and senescence. He describes senescence as assuming similar form in each species as evidenced by the physicochemical changes in collagen, the incidence of vascular degeneration or the high incidence of cancer, the whole gamut of events being guided by a genetic 'programme in time'

THE TRANS-SCIENCE ASPECTS OF DISEASE AND DEATH

specific to each species.

Van der Leeuw, talking in a similar vein as Burnet, states that we are time, we are timed, we are the timer. 'We are temporal... The man of nine thirty is not the same as the man of nine twenty five'. The most important point in the foregoing regarding man's disease and dying is the apparently sweeping generalization that the man two and half minutes ago is not the same as the man two and a half minutes later. This bold generalization carries with it the ability to resolve many a paradox witnessed in modern medical practice – the puzzle, for example, of a person just dropping dead while full of life, or soon after being given a clean bill of health.

Nelson Rockefeller, 'the richest man in the world,' dropped dead, 'working at his desk', at the age of 70. The press particularly added that 'Mr. Rockefeller had no history of heart trouble and he used to joke with his children that he was going to live up to a hundred years.' Dean Acheson, the former American Secretary of State, died in a similar manner: 'Full of years and honors, he slumped forward on his desk, without a moment's agony or suspense.' Pope Paul IV suffered a heart attack while resting in bed, and soon died. The deceased Pope was replaced by John Paul I, who died a bare 33 days after his appointment, probably from a massive stroke he suffered in his sleep. Winston Churchill's wife died of a heart attack, at 92, while eating lunch at her London home. Similarly, Charles de Gaulle: 'One neighbor had seen him in the afternoon on business and had come away feeling that *le vieux* was in superb health. At a few minutes past seven in the evening, he was about to sit down and thumb through some papers and perhaps play a game of patience. He merely had time to clutch his side and gasp, "It hurts", before collapsing. The doctor was summoned, as was the local priest who administered the last rites. Less than two weeks before his 80th birthday, Charles de Gaulle was dead from a ruptured blood vessel.' The fact that all these deaths occurred to individuals who were resting, relaxing, or relaxedly working gives the lie to the medical theory of some 'stress' as the basis of such deaths.

It may be argued that the above group comprised aged people who did not take enough exercise. Opie and others, in *The New England Journal of Medicine* described the deaths from heart attack, in a boy of 19½ and a man of 35, both accomplished athletes in the peak of physical fitness. LES, 49, a surgeon in South Dakota, died following a cerebral hemorrhage while he was operating on a patient. SG, a surgeon studying for his Fellowship in London, died of a heart attack at 29.

The sudden, unanticipated death from heart attack of say, Rockefeller at 70, and DLK, an orthopaedic surgeon, at 30, both fighting fit and with no history of heart trouble, cannot be related convincingly to any anatomical, physiological, pathological, or genetic factors. Many a person with any or all the presumed predisposing factors, even to a more severe degree, carries on admirably well, regardless, to eventually die unexpectedly and inexplicably of something else. Rockefeller died at 70, DLK at 30, incidentally of heart attack, both ages falling well within the age distribution of heart attack and resultant death, or of overall human mortality. A death hormone has been postulated; a death mechanism obeying an individual's timer may be operative, doing what it wants to and when, and giving a disease a bad name. In an analysis of the death-rates in four major diseases by Zumoff and others, the startling finding was that the death-rate was neither related to the severity of the disease nor to its earliness or lateness, but to some undefined physiological systems governed solely by the passage of time.

What really killed all these people, and would kill most of us, is not this disease or that, but the fact, ascertainable only *a posteriori,* that the time was up, as declared by a timer inside. The allegorical timer inside is a pointer to the fact that, as of today, modern medicine can talk about *the time of death* of anyone healthy, diseased or more diseased, only after the death has occurred. No list of predisposing factors including the medical prognosis of doom nor the findings at the anachronistic clinicopathological conferences allow a tenable correlation between the medical data and the why and when of death. It is the subservience of death to time alone as determined by the

THE TRANS-SCIENCE ASPECTS OF DISEASE AND DEATH

timer inside that allows a Tito or a Karen Ann Quinlan to tick on and on in the teeth of adverse opinion of medical experts, and a de Gaulle or Acheson to slump down dead when medically least expected to do so. We are time; we are ended by time.

Dobzhansky speaking from a biologist's point of view talks of death as the climax of our proportioned and programmed development. Ageing, diseasing, senescence and death are held as built-in processes mediating biological maturation consisting of a series of gradual changes through time from conception to death. 'To die, a man needs no disease. When the time is up, he dies with disease or without, regardless of full health and vigour. Like a ripened fruit falling off a tree on its own, man passes away on getting the call from the inner clock. People often wonder: "Oh, he was happy, healthy, active, and yet he died!"'. (Bhave) Death reigns, indifferent to the thousand man-made ifs and buts. The healthy may not survive, the diseased may not die.

Vinoba Bhave's aphorism explains why people, in the pink of health and in the prime of their life, die a 'natural death,' and people who are manifestly afflicted with a major disease, or diseases not only drag on, but even seem to thrive. Leonid Brezhnev ruled the roost despite a rich assortment of chronic illnesses – gout, leukemia, emphysema, cardio-vascular problems needing a pacemaker, and also, possibly a jaw cancer, brain tumor, and chronic pneumonia. Golda Meir, the 'tough maternal, legend,' already had a lymphoma when she became the premier in 1969. It took her cancer 13 years before she succumbed to its 'complications' at the age of 80. Many a person afflicted with medically certified 'killer diseases' survives long enough to falsify the prognosis of doom.

The best example of the above is offered by an experimental study in the United States. In order to study the development of major diseases in relation to age in rats, Simms and co-workers created ideal animal quarters which, because they offered the test animals board and lodging, comparable to a Waldorf-Astoria, came to be known as the Rat Palace. Visitors who had come in contact with other rats elsewhere were strictly forbidden in order to preclude the possibility of their transferring any contagious disease to the rats in the Rat Palace. And yet in this rat-utopia, diseases and death occurred with predictable timing and frequency. Comparing the findings of this experiment on rats with those in man, the authors concluded that, barring the differences in the time scale, the findings on rats were easily applicable to man and that the factors that determine longevity (or mortality) of the two species seemed to operate in a closely comparable fashion. Needless to say, the diseases in rats bore the same relation to death, as in man: death and disease occurred independent of each other. This comparison between rat and man brings us to the next important factor – namely, relativity.

Relativity

For several criteria of *relative time*, all mammals live about the same span. All mammals, for example, breathe about the same number of times in their lives. The problems of middle and old age that bother man do not spare the animals. Most spontaneous cancers in animals, as in man, occur in middle-aged or elderly animals. It is also true of atherosclerosis, be it man, swine or killer whale. These observations and the Rat Palace experiments of Simms and his co-workers drive home the relativistic nature of animal/human senescence and death. Collagen, although physicochemically similar in man, horse, dog, rat and mouse, exhibits maximal, and very closely comparable, age-changes in these animals respectively at 70, 25, 12, 3 and 2 years. Thus man, in terms of ageing and death, is a mouse whose time scale has been enlarged 35 times.

The relativity that prevails at the collagen-level, disease-level, and lifespan-level, is clearly reflected in the number of times the embryonic cells can multiply – the upper limit of the capacity being known as the Hayflick limit. Hayflick has demonstrated that the duplicating capacity of the cells from the embryo of an animal relates closely to its lifespan – the greater the lifespan, the greater is the number of times the cells can serially multiply.

We now have sufficient information to reach an understanding of the *relativity* of biological lifespan. Although the cells and the collagen fibers of all mammals are very similar, they age at a rate that is inversely proportional to their lifespan. Further, given the time-adjustment between different species (that is 3 years for a rat corresponds to 70 years for man), both the cells and the collagen fibers reach the same endpoint in all mammalian species. In terms of cells and fibers (cytofibernetics), we are forced to conclude that man is no more than $70/2$ or $70/12$ times a longer lived mouse or dog respectively. Man's ageing is relatively slow, that of the dog less slow, that of the mouse slower still. The rates differ, but not the basic style. The problem is, strictly, one of relativity. Jacqueline Susann, in a novel about her dog Josephine presents this relativity in the most telling manner:

> She said, 'That's a cute puppy you've got. How old is it?'
> I said 'Six.'
> 'But she is forty-two years old,' the woman insisted. Who was forty-two? Even Josephine looked interested. Josephine was forty-two, the woman insisted. A dog's life is seven to our one. At six, Josie was forty-two. A middle-aged woman.

Such differing rates of ageing are seen even within the human herd, where, despite the genetic similarity of one man to another, one lives for 19 years the other for 91 years, one grays earlier and the other later, one woman gets cancer and the other escapes, and so on. The basis of these differences lies in the bioforce of *normality* as governs a given herd. While relativity explains the differences between species, normality underlies the differences within a species.

Normality

To say what things are normal, one must know what is abnormal. Alas, medicine has not been able to define what constitutes *the* normal, be it the blood sugar or the blood pressure. It is high time that normal/normality is accorded its pristine status of a field-concept that is thoroughly irrelevant and inapplicable at an individual level.

The current widespread problem concerning the normal and normality is traceable to carpentry, geometry, and arithmetic. *Norma* means the carpenter's square, and hence in geometry, *normal* connotes perpendicular, as also a line perpendicular to the tangent to the point of a curve. By extension, normal implies the point at which this perpendicular line intercepts the X-axis. Since in a Gaussian curve, this point of interception falls on the arithmetic average on the X-axis, normal is regarded as synonymous with *mean* or *average* and everything to its right or left becomes *deviation, error,* or what is worse, *abnormal.* The etymological errors multiply to equate 'normal' with 'sane, natural, prevalent, regular, typical' and by virtue of all this, 'ideal'. In this jungle of verbal distortions, what has been lost sight of is the fact that the appellation 'normal' refers to a form of frequency distribution, also called Gaussian distribution. Such a distribution provides a graph or a curve that is bell-shaped, symmetrical, with its two ends stretchable to infinity, thus allowing the widest variations of a parameter, say, blood pressure readings, to fall within normality. The law of normality prevails in the inanimate sphere with as much felicity as in the animate world.

Any biological characteristic that can be measured, exhibits normal distribution. This could be human birth weight, under conditions 'normal' or 'abnormal', blood cholesterol levels, or intelligence. Must it not be for reasons of normality that the brain size varies widely on either side of the mythical normal (that is to say average) brain, with Anatole France enjoying a mere half of the brain size of Lord Byron or Oliver Cromwell, with Einstein in between, near the average? Again, would not the normality of distribution of intelligence, independent of the brain size, account for the brightness of Anatole France, the genius of Einstein and the mental retardation of individuals with oversized brains?

If physiological features such as blood pressure or acid secretion in the stomach exhibit normality in their distribution, pathological features – even of the most serious nature – are no less normally distributed. In any population, it is the normality

THE TRANS-SCIENCE ASPECTS OF DISEASE AND DEATH

of distribution of the so-called pathological traits that determines the occurrence, severity, age at diagnosis, post-diagnostic/post-treatment survival, or the age at death, of such diverse diseases as congenital malformations, peptic ulcer, hypertension, diabetes mellitus, cancer, heart attack, etc.

The discussion on normality can be concluded with the realization that each of the many features, physiological or pathological, that comprises a human being, is unpredictably and unalterably distributed on the normal curve, independent of all other features. To the utter chagrin of modern medicine and its specialists, such a 'normal' state of affairs makes *uncertain* the what, when, why of every disease, forcing modern medicine to be plagued by uncertainty at the level of the individual patient. Let us now understand the fourth element, namely, uncertainty.

Uncertainty

Uncertainty, the *alter ego* of Pascalian probability, is the child of normality, the science of quantitative differences between human beings. Modern medicine, without doubt, has spawned a gargantuan technocracy, unmindful of the quantitative nature of all human differences – anatomical, physiological, psychic, pathologic or thanatologic. The seemingly gross differences between two persons – one with elementary intelligence the other with creative genius, one with high stomach acid and no ulcer the other with low acid and ulcer, one surviving cancer, the other succumbing to it, and so on – are all a matter of quantitative variations normally distributed throughout the species.

In health and in disease, human beings differ, one from another, but the difference that modern medicine can detect, given its most sophisticated gadgetry, is not qualitative, but quantitative, not one of character but of measurement. Human beings quantitatively differ very widely, this being the nature of any parameter normally distributed. And there is no way of telling which human being, healthy or diseased, would show what reading, and why. This makes for the nagging uncertainty that modern medicine can not dispel while dealing with an individual patient.

It is the uncertainty principle which lends medical practice its mysterious element of unpredictability that charms and challenges the man of action – the medical man. It is uncertainty, backed by temporality and normality that accounts for an esophagus declared normal today but found cancerous tomorrow and ECG (EKG) being assured as all right today, and worrisome tomorrow, the patient given up as lost today, surviving to attend his physician's funeral, tomorrow. But for uncertainty, medical practice would not have been half as fascinating.

Summing up

Time, uncertainty, relativity and normality universally govern development, disease and death – concepts that allow an intellectual ratiocination of both the trans-science and trans-medicine aspects of disease and death.

These concepts have some wider implications for modern medicine. They put modern medicine in its place, dismissing as naive modern medicine's causalism – fat causes heart attack, coitus causes cancer. These concepts further promise to cure modern medicine of its characteristic obsession that every ill – congenital or acquired – is a preventable outcome of some molecular, genetic or cytological aberration. The borderlines that modern medicine has created stand erased, for we realize that the difference between the 'normal' and the 'abnormal' is not that between black and white but between shades of gray, with no dividing line anywhere. The phenomenon of death acquires the status of an independent, physiological function: we are purposely, unalterably programmed to die. All major problems – congenital, cardiovascular, cancerous, or metabolic – that medicine is claiming to be intensely researching upon, are, in essence, unresearchable. Science etymologically means *knowing*, not *doing*. Disease and death are not trans-science if we aim to understand them. They are so only if we want to manipulate them. More correctly, aren't they trans-technique?

The choicest implication of this chapter, however may be its

THE TRANS-SCIENCE ASPECTS OF DISEASE AND DEATH

integration of physical laws and biological laws, physicists and physicians, matter and man. By hinting at the integral relationship between time, relativity and uncertainty – hitherto only in the domain of matter – and man, the borderline between the living and non-living grows fainter. In the telling words of Ardrey, 'Time and death and the space between the stars – these are the ingredients of the woman who prepares your breakfast, or of the man who gets off the train as you get on.' This chapter amplifies a poetic insight in order to put into place laws that may govern you, the person who prepares your breakfast, as also the men you meet in the street. It's but a peremptory perspective on the democracy, the immense impartiality, the trans-science temper, the Upanishad or the Tao of human development, disease and death.

CHAPTER 6 The Trans-Technique Aspects of Disease and Death

> This is the century, we are told, in which innovation and scientific-technological advance – progress in other words – should be able to produce anything within the limits of what is physically possible in principle. We have only to want it sufficiently and to pay the price and we can have it. If rocks from the moon can be brought to Houston, why should we not be able to apply molecular biology, cytology, and the rest, to cure what is now incurable?
>
> MacFarlane Burnet

The technological triumphs in medicine this century outweigh and outclass the aggregate achievements of the entire human past; yet modern man has been denied the elixir, the cure for his disease and death. An objective survey of medicine's failures reveals that it is not that the technology *per se* is ineffective – it does what it is designed to do – but that what technology solves is trivial, and what it just cannot touch is crucial, being beyond *any* technique – extant, evolving, or envisaged. Most of human diseasing and death is trans-technique.

What is *technique*, and what is *trans-technique*? Technique in medicine is whatever a doctor does to a patient, be it diagnosing, treating or prognosing. It admits of the simplest to the superlatively sophisticated. *Trans-technique* aspects of disease and death are those innate, ordinary, day-to-day features of human diseasing and dying that *technique* can in no way modify to a patient's advantage. Before we detail the principles that underlie the trans-technique-ness, a survey of the state of the medical art at the end of this century is in order.

THE TRANS-TECHNIQUE ASPECTS OF DISEASE AND DEATH

'Need your doctor be so useless?'

The above title of a book by the Canadian physician A. Malleson is symptomatic of the current state of modern medicine – confronted with congenital malformations, cancer, coronary artery disease, peripheral artery disease, stroke, high blood pressure, or diabetes.

'It is a sobering thought that after several decades of research, a number of international conferences and many other meetings, seminars and symposia, the problem of human malformations remains essentially unchanged.' Having introduced a symposium with these words, McKeown proceeds to chastise modern medicine further on human malformations – etiology unknown, rate unchanged, relative contribution to infant mortality greatly increased.

Breast cancer, as a paradigm, typifies the colossal failure of cancer research: It is a subcutaneaous (under-the-skin, superficial) cancer – the natural history of which has been studied for the past 200 years at least, easily amenable to examination by the patient herself, and more so by the doctor, subjected to varied forms of grading, staging, radiography, hormonal therapy, minimal to most radical surgery, and cocktails of chemotherapy – that has stubbornly refused to yield at all, in *any* way from the time a group of Scottish physicians published a memorandum on its nature in 1802. Indeed, Atkins of England pointed out that the recent studies on breast cancer have made such tremendous progress that, today, no one knows how to treat it.

Coronary artery disease, generally manifest as heart attack, has been attacked by doctors through electronic wizardry enshrined in the ICCU's and through a work of surgical excellence called the coronary bypass. Of no avail. The ICCU's, wryly described as 'pressure cookers' have proved counterproductive, with the patient having a greater chance of dying there than outside. McIntosh, a past president of the American College of Cardiology commented on coronary bypass that 'there is no convincing evidence that the procedure prevents or postpones premature death.' Datey, a leading Indian cardiologist stated: 'The five year end results of heart patients with conservative medical treatment and bypass surgery are the same.'

About peripheral artery diseases, Jaffe has observed: 'Despite an extraordinary investment in research resources we are still far from understanding the pathologic mechanisms responsible for peripheral vascular diseases. As a consequence, all treatment, medical and surgical, must be directed toward abatement of symptoms and prevention of complications, rather than against the diseases themselves. It must be clear, therefore, that our therapeutic armamentarium is limited severely.'

Stroke, medically labelled as cerebrovascular disease, has remained impervious to all modes of medical management, maintaining its pristine behaviour the world-over, exercising closely comparable 5-year-survival rates and 'funeral-rates', prompting an epidemiologist to suggest that we had better accept it as but a form of ageing, being as unsolvable and as irreversible as ageing itself.

High blood pressure, medically called *essential hypertension* or *essential high blood pressure,* has remained an elusive entity for it has yet to be defined, satisfactorily for the doctor or rewardingly for the patient. Pickering, one time Regius professor of medicine at Oxford, showed that the 'so-called essential hypertension' is incapable of being defined except arbitrarily, the definition varying from day to day, doctor to doctor, and place to place. Doctors cannot decide whether or not what they call high blood pressure or hypertension is something natural to the patient, being 'a disease in its own right;' and no wonder, they hold the appellation *essential,* as essential to their hypertensive thinking. As is the definition, so too are the diagnosis, treatment, and prognosis of essential hypertension – arbitrary, erratic and anxiety-making.

Talking of diabetes, Boyd, an eminent pathologist and author, lamented that the more we know about it the less we seem to understand it. This continuing counterproductiveness stems from the fact that (a) diabetes – more completely called diabetes mellitus – has never been clearly defined, (b) the disturbances of glucose metabolism that doctors emphasize and treat represent only the tip of the iceberg of the disturbed metabolism of the patient, and (c) neither insulin nor any other 'antidiabetic' agent alters the course of the disease or the accompanying, inevitable arterial damage. It is chastizing to note that 60 years after the epochal discovery of insulin and its (first) usage on Leonard Thompson, we know more about the inherent limitations of insulin therapy than about its presumed ability to 'cure' diabetes.

All told, the most sophisticated medical manoeuvers or machines don't seem to make a major difference, and 'advances in diagnosis and treatment do not necessarily translate into increased survival.' Most of the tools a doctor used twenty-five years ago fitted into a small black bag; today the technologically-armed physician owns or has access to $250,000 worth of equipment; whenever one tries to link the development of new technology with a coincidental improvement in healing, the answer is always the same: Nil. Medical recourse to computers has had the the GIGO snag: Garbage In, Garbage Out.

Where has medical technology gone wrong? A dispassionate, epistemological evaluation of medicine's technological gains reveals them to be *imagery, accessible, analytic, associative,* and *amplificatory.* The more the physicistic science and the physicianly art interact, the greater is the variety of means by which medical imagery can be obtained. Yet, to take but one example, X-rays, xeroradiography and computerized-tomgraphic (CT) scan, ultrasonography and nuclear-magnetic-resonance (NMR) imaging have left a cancer where it was – diagnosed a little too late. The ability to cannulate the pancreatic duct or artery towards the diagnosis and treatment of pancreatic cancer, or to get into the skull to treat brain cancer, is an accessible advance that leaves the cancer's autonomy untouched. Increasingly refined biochemical techniques allow many a substance to be measured with *pico*-precision (pico $=1/10^{12}$), thus analytically telling us a lot about heart attack, diabetes mellitus or rheumatoid arthritis, but without the liberty to predictably and/or favourably alter the course of the disease. Epidemiology connects the husband's cigar to the wife's cancer, coffee to cardiovascular disease, and refined sugar to peptic ulcer – an associative exercise that makes more anxiety than sense. The electron microscope amplifies the size of a T-lymphocyte any number of times only to amplify our ignorance of the cell to the same magnitude. In modern medicine, technology glisters, but is, often, not gold.

A number of diverse medical men have admitted that ninety per cent of the bad things that happen to man's body are beyond the ken of modern medicine. Armed with technical might, the doctor can, with the healing power of nature providentially at the patient's beck and call, revert acute physiological crises to healthy states, set fractures, fix retinae, deliver babies facing a narrow birth canal, remove lumps and cataracts, replace a valve or a joint, correct mechanical defects such as cleft palate or hernia, all this comprising the ten per cent of man's maladies that medicine *can* manage. The rest is trans-technique. Let us see how, and why.

Four principles account for the trans-technique nature of diseases. These are *cellularity, systemicity, uniqueness* and *herdity*. An integrated appreciation of these principles will help us understand medicine's limits, no matter what its technical might.

Cellularity

There are features of a mammalian cell that make disease and death trans-technique in more ways than one. It is a fitting paradox that what advanced cytological techniques have revealed about the cell has driven home the truth that a cell's behavior, in health or disease, can hardly be trifled with.

The microsize of human body cells accounts for the fact that before a scan discovers a cancerous lump measuring one cubic millimeter and weighing one milligram – the smallest tumor mass that one could ever hope to detect clinically – the cancer is already a million cells strong and several years old. Early diagnosis of cancer is, thus, only a myth. The same considerations apply to the disease of coronary (or any other) arteries, the underlying atheromatous process being held by some as cancerous in origin. Any attempt at flooding the body with anti-abnormal cell-agents (radiation, chemicals) fails because of the selfsameness of all body cells, rendering selective destruction of undesired cells impossible. Supposing that a highly specific drug is developed and administered, the target cell can easily recall its microbial past to readjust its genetic machinery – that is, mutate – to knock out the drug, since the mutative repertoire of a human cell borders on 256 followed by 2.4 billion zeros.

In no two human beings, twins not excluded, do the cells of one see eye-to-eye with those of the other person. Each cell, then, in a human being, has an irrepressible *individuality* that brooks no foreign cell around nor is likely to be tolerated as friend in an alien body. This is an age of transplants, performed because they are technically easy, although biologically baseless. Following any organ/cell transplant, the donor cells and guest cells wage a relentless war for which the patient (the recipient) pays a great price. There is nothing on the medical horizon that can mitigate the biological impotence of organ transplantation.

Systemicity

The human body is an integrated whole that starts as a single cell, and builds up a cytogalaxy that behaves as a single, concerted unit whose seemingly disparate parts form, grow, and decay in unison. Systemicity of a disease implies its presence in wide areas of the body. Cancer, for example, has been correctly declared a disease of the whole organism. Arteriosclerosis or the hardening-and-blocking of the body's arteries involves all the areas of the body. Diabetes (mellitus) affects all blood vessels and all parts of the metabolic machinery of the individual. All diseases of ageing involve the whole body; they thus exhibit systemicity.

The systemicity of a disease rules out its being either diagnosed early or removed or destroyed completely. A cancer thus does not lend itself to complete destruction by surgery, radiation, chemotherapy, or immunotherapy. Even if we were to nab the last cancer cell, the next normal cell would foil attempts by turning cancerous, through a process named *neocanceration* or *recruitment*. The sole curative triumph against gestational choriocarcinoma (a cancer arising from fetal tissue during pregnancy) is entirely due to the fact that such an eventuality of neocanceration is ruled out by the absence of the normal progenitor cells that comprise the discarded fetal part of the placenta. An arterial bypass takes care of the block that the operator sees or has access to, but what of the arteries beyond, or before, or elsewhere? This explains why a patient with heart disease fails to benefit from the much-vaunted coronary artery bypass. As for diabetes, antidiabetic agents touch the proverbial tip of the metabolic iceberg, affecting in no way the overall, arterial disease and fat and protein metabolic disorders, that are now accepted as integral parts of the diabetic process.

Uniqueness

Variability, it is said, is the only invariable law of biology, a natural propensity that unfailingly varies one cancer from another, one heart attack from the next. If the uniqueness of every individual is an unsolved problem of biology, then the uniqueness of every disease is the unsolved and unsolvable problem of medicine. There are as many different diseases as patients. Even 'identical' twins differ in their individual disease patterns. The presumed identicality of the genotype in such twins is unable to circumvent this code of individuality.

Cancer, indisputably traceable to precisely pinpointable and culturable cancer cells, provides a remarkable example of the unprecedented, unparalleled and unrepeatable nature of a disease. Naturally occurring cancers are extremely diverse even when they carry the same diagnostic label. No two cases of coronary artery disease, stroke, cancer, diabetes, arthritis or auto-immune disease are identical either in their presentation or in their progress. The behavioral uniqueness of a disease, with its unpredictability, forms the basis for unexpected successes and equally unexpected failures, given the same treatment. Cancers have been classified into 'good' and 'bad', the good ones curable

THE TRANS-TECHNIQUE ASPECTS OF DISEASE AND DEATH

by any treatment, the bad ones by none – a retroactive judgment applicable to any other disease and fully justifying the Chinese proverb that a therapy works in a patient destined to survive.

This proverb smacks of irreverence for the celebrated and seemingly learned art of prognosing, now backed up by technology. Among diagnosis, prognosis and treatment, prognosis is the most difficult to evaluate. The accurate prediction of things to come is baffling, perplexing, and problematic. The reason is two-fold: (a) In most diseases, what the doctors can prognosticate about is based on group statistics that obviously have no bearing on an individual case. (b) Even when, at an individual level, the doctor has fully at hand the reports of some test, ECG (EKG), X-ray, or scan, and thus 'justifiably' bases his prognosis on the evident benignity or otherwise of the lesion, such a correlation has not proved trustworthy or fruitful. Patients with reassuring investigations and prognosis have died, and those with a prognosis of doom have survived. All technological marvels, computers not excluded, deal with the appearances and assumed correlations of a human being's disease; none, as yet, knows or can know of the behavioral uniqueness of such a biological entity. Of diagnosis, treatment, and prognosis, the last is the most trans-technique.

The unique reality of medical practice is that, be it Paul Dudley White (Cardiologist to American Presidents) and his 103 year old patient Charles Thierry, or James Herriot and the dog Jock, it is a one-to-one encounter where the uniqueness of the individual, his disease, his very biological trajectory is unpredictable, unalterable, and overwhelmingly important. For modern medicine, the most chastizing part of an individual's biological trajectory is its refusal to provide any quantitative correlationship between the earliness or lateness of a disease on the one hand, and the probability of the disease and/or death on the other. The healthy do not necessarily survive; the diseased do not necessarily die. Norman Cousins' dig at medical experts who 'don't really know enough' in his *Anatomy of an Illness* must be viewed from the standpoint that the experts never know anywhere near enough, not because they do not want to, but because what they wish to know and what patients expect them to be knowledgeable about truly lies in the realm of the unknown, or, more accurately, unknowable.

Herdity

Herdity could well be described, at the very outset, as a corporate programme subserved by individual performance. Cellularity, systemicity and uniqueness are features innate to an individual; herdity is a force that the human herd exerts on the individual. The relationship between the individual and the herd is a remarkable biological feature that more than vindicates John Donne's statement that 'no man is an island of itself: every man is a part of the main.'

Mankind was, and is, a single inclusive population and is endowed with a single corporate genotype, a single gene pool. Appropriate to this is the concept of an individual as one who extends, in time as in space, beyond the frontiers of his body, and who is linked to the past and to the future, regardless of the ephemerality of his present. Add to this the conceptual framework of quantum physics that reveals a basic oneness of the universe in which, at a deep and fundamental level, the seemingly separate parts of the universe are connected in an intimate and immediate way, in a complicated web of relations between the various parts of the whole. We are now poised to view an individual's body, his disease, his cancer – each unfailingly unique – as a spatiotemporal manifestation of a cosmic order. I am what I am, and allowed to be so, for I know who all others were, are, and will be so as not to duplicate them, and they in turn know of me so as not to make a duplicate of me or of my disease at any time.

Climbing down from cosmic considerations to clinical, bedside reality allows us to appreciate the role of herdity in distribution of disease in any given group. As general statistics go, the incidence of, say, acute lymphatic leukemia is 1 in 33,000, of cleft palate or neural tube defect is 1 in less than 1,000, of cancer 1 in 5, of blood vessel disease 1 in 2, at random, country

THE TRANS-TECHNIQUE ASPECTS OF DISEASE AND DEATH

after country, year after year. A surveyor of the statistical figures on the occurrence of cancer is struck by their unexpected constancy, for a given region, year after year, decade after decade. A high incidence of cancer in one part of the body is consistently balanced for a given country or a population, by a low incidence of cancer at another site, to permit the reassuring generalization that cancer occurs everywhere in the world, in excess nowhere. The age-specific mortality rates from cardio-vascular disease, year after year, decade after decade, and in country after country fit quite closely the same line. There is a fundamental natural benevolence in the global impartiality with which disease and death treat mankind. The prevalence of diabetes mellitus is more or less constant for all countries. Cancer, stroke, diabetes, hypertension, heart attack and so on are an integral part of humanity, of human herdity. This remarkable herd-certainty and individual probability of pathological events is a function of a corporate herd program that finds expression at the level of an individual who has crossed a critical genetic threshold. Herdity, thus, is a reciprocal relationship between an individual and his herd, what geneticists have been describing as polygenic inheritance.

The evolution of the concept of polygenic inheritance has brought a shift in genetic thinking, from heredity to herdity, for polygenic inheritance is necessarily a statistical concept that concerns not the individual but popualtion aggregates. Polygenic inheritance has been invoked to explain a wide variety of diseases, ranging from congenital malformations to cancer, porphyria to peptic ulcer. This means that most diseases do not have a cause. Causeless diseases cannot be prevented; they are an integral part of man's growth; in terms of both cause and course they are trans-technique. Herdity is trans-technique.

The idea of herdity governs all the phenomena in relation to disease and death in a herd. The herd determines who will get what and when, in whom the disease will be slow, in whom fast, and so on. This would explain why the commonness of prostatic cancer beyond the age of 50 is paradoxically matched by the uncommonness of its malignant behavior and how persons with bad coronary angiograms survive those with good ones.

The most compelling evidence in favor of herdity is, in general, the programmed, herd mortality that, as a physiological function, is seen in man, in animals, and in drosophila. Gompertz saw this as a constant increment in mortality beyond the third quinquennium of human life, doubling every 8 years, a phenomenon no medical advance has been able to stem. John Knowles, as president of the Rockefeller Foundation, wrote in 1977 on 'The responsibility of an individual' charging the latter's 'personal misbehavior and environmental conditions' for over ninety-nine percent of illnesses. Knowles' faith in reasoned behavior did not prevent the pancreatic cancer that killed him in 1979. He was but one of the 19,000 that develop pancreatic cancer and die from it in the United States every year. Knowles died at 52, some do at an earlier age, others at a later age, all a part of herd distribution, of herdity.

Summing up

Lester Brown, of the Worldwatch Institute, has divided recent history into two distinct technological periods – the period 1940 to 1970 of unrestrained optimism, the second, thereafter, of utter disillusionment, of the crumbling of a seemingly shatter-proof faith in technology. It is time that medical men understand the reason behind this stalemate, and turn the situation to the benefit of their patients and to their own enlightenment.

Cellularity, systemicity, uniqueness and herdity can be realized as the *suchness*, of diseasing and dying. The evolution of the trans-technique concept explains technology's failures and limits, exercises restraints on this age of inflated expectations, encourages us to be radical enough to abjure straight-line solutions and many a technological trap – to wit, the tyranny of mass-screening, debilitating therapies, or kill-joy preventionism.

An editorial in *The New England Journal of Medicine* entitled 'The toss-up' bears eloquent testimony to the rationale of the above. It is common experience that, on a given case, the proposed diagnostic or therapeutic thrust ranges from extreme conservatism to surgical ultra-radicalism. After attributing such

THE TRANS-TECHNIQUE ASPECTS OF DISEASE AND DEATH

divergence in medical thinking to the idiosyncracies of the physicians, the authors propose: 'Perhaps all these factors are involved in clinical controversies, but we propose that one explanation has not been sufficiently recognized: that it simply makes no difference which choice is made. We suggest that some dramatic controversies represent "toss-ups" – clinical situations in which the consequences of divergent choices are, on the average, virtually identical.' The identicality of the consequences, no matter what the investigations and what the therapy, is a result of the basic fact that the problem being tackled is beyond the limits of technology.

Scientis est potentia: knowledge is power. The knowledge that a lot in medical practice is beyond medical technique can, as a concept, propel us towards discerning inaction in medicine. Munsif, an eminent Bombay surgeon, was fond of stating that 'a good surgeon is one who knows when not to operate.' What a medical man needs to learn, in today's technicalized scene is when *not* to act, an intellectual and a therapeutic revolution that can safely rest on the concept of trans-technique.

The well-informed physician and patient of tomorrow will accept 'doing nothing' as an integral part of the relevant investigations, diagnosis, and treatment. No treatment can often be the right treatment, a proposition that is consistent with a revised connotation of 'cure', the most cherished word in medicine. The word 'cure' comes from *curatio* 'I take care'. Jackson, Oliver Wendell Holmes' teacher, never talked of curing a patient except in the true sense of 'taking care'. Jackson felt that doctors, by the misuse of the word 'cure' arrogated to themselves greater powers than were their due. Modern medicine is in need of humility, and must restore 'cure' to its pristine and most pertinent meaning: with a concerned physician around, no disease, no death, is incurable. A drug to ease, a procedure to palliate, a word of cheer, the graceful stoicism to hold the dying patient's hand – all this and more falls within the curative comptence of a compassionate clinician. Regardless of the trans-science and the trans-technique aspects of disease and death, the art of medicine and the *Dear and Glorious Physician,* will be there forever.

CHAPTER 7 The Dictates of the Nature of Disease and Death

What's my turn today
may be thine tomorrow.

Doctor Thomas Fuller

Disease and death are probabilistic *herd* functions that at random express themselves at an individual level. In any herd, at a given time, *all* can disease or die. Only some do. An understanding of disease and death can inspire humility and gratitude when one is alive and healthy, fortitude when one is diseased or dying, and compassion when one is a witness to these.

And who that is alive is not facing death? The democratic operations of death make for each one of us, *death here and now*, an inescapable reality that spells, again for each one of us, *life* in its fullest, richest intensity – *here and now*. Our civilization's 'abdication of ecstasy' is rooted in our ostrich-like disregard for the sandstorms of our inner, biological time that spell now and again, disease and death. Up to now we have been blind to the democracy of disease and death.

Dictates of the democracy of disease

1. All *-isms* apart, one man's disease – congenital, cancerous, vascular, metabolic, even infectious, and traumatic – is an expression of (bio)socialism, that is governed by a social contract. A *Dictionary of Modern Thought* defines socialism as a social system based on common ownership of the means of production and distribution. A herd, a society, by its corporate genotype owns and produces a birth defect, a stroke or a cancer and distributes it to some individuals at random, on an impartial and probabilistic basis. The dictionary further defines 'social

contract' as the unwritten agreement between the members of a society to behave with reciprocal responsibility in their relationship, under the governance of the 'State' which, in social contract theory, is presupposed by the existence of that society.

The corollaries to the above are concise and clear: One man's cancer is another four men's freedom from it; my severe diabetes is because of the mildness or absence of your diabetes; my child's cleft-palate allows another 999 children to escape it; one person's acute lymphoblastic leukemia ensures the freedom of 32,999 persons from it. The force of normality ordains that the distribution of intelligence in a herd will entail two per cent as mentally backward to balance the IQ scores in the top two percent, IQ being a herd function governed by polygenes. The top brass in the echelons of IQ and creativity owe a 'normal' debt to the rest. Every healthy, disease-free individual carries with her or him an IOU card addressed to another individual not so gifted.

'"Your son has acute appendicitis, I'm afraid. We must discuss the fee for the operation. Can you afford twenty guineas?" That question from a surgeon, put to parents living near London in 1938, might well stand as the sole justification for the creation in Britain, ten years later, of a structure of medical care which strove to divorce the urgency of a patient's need from his ability to pay for the treatment.' This editorial comment in *The Lancet* of 1972 has undiminished relevance today, the world over. The fee-for-service principle breeds the twin anomalies of (a) service rendered, *only if* the patient's purse is full, and (b) service rendered, *often needlessly*, just because the patient or the insurance company can pay. Both are antithetic to the socialism and social contract that govern disease and death in any society.

2. Disease, as a personal event, is not to be treated with self-pity, for such a feeling has a tendency to expand out of all proportion. As diseasing is inherent to growing, a disease must be lived with, with life and business as usual. If there is disease, that is what ought to be treated.

3. Paralyzing, corrosive pity for the diseased – a behavioral norm

in modern society – is summarily unjustified: (a) the pitied may outlive the pitier; (b) the presence of disease is no prohibition against a good, creative, full life; (c) the pity stemming from a healthier-than-thou attitude can serve no useful purpose.

Cornelius Ryan, the author of best selling World War II trilogy, died of cancer. But before the cancer could kill him, his friends almost did: 'Well, we really can't ask Ryan to do this article or count on him to finish this book, because the poor bastard's got cancer.' Modern society has been nurtured on the concept of disease as a product of faulty living, an *idée fixe* that is pregnant with the unmistakable ring of an accusation. Ryan, alientated from ordinary life, used to be greeted by the silence of his friends that made him feel as if he had committed 'some unpardonable gaffe'.

4. It cannot be overemphasized that, quite contrary to medical scare-mongering but much in conformity with the laws of the herd, a disease tends to remain silent for long, even right up to death, and the discomfort that it may produce does not necessarily mean death or even early death from that malady.

5. The health and vigour of the young, in any herd or nation, is in direct proportion to the number of aged people it has. The West has been a self-evident example of this for a long time and East is catching up. While the expediencies of job scarcity force the message '65 and out', the same has nothing to do with the right to full living, creativity, sex, and what is most important, respect. The doctors' own lack of contact with the realities of ageing of a herd is sadly reflected in their talking of the elderly as 'old crocks', and in their penchant for making a fast buck from the problems of the aged.

The cult of youth is ignorant of the time dimension, of the fact that the old can and do outlive and outperform younger people, and that the greater number of the elderly only reflects a much greater number heading for that oldness. The pathetic lack of awareness of this truth has fostered prejudices and predispositions against old age. This irreverence toward the old – *ageism* – can only be changed by substantial doses of reality. It is time to

THE DICTATES OF THE NATURE OF DISEASE AND DEATH

revive the Eastern and the Navajo tradition of revering the aged. It is a necessary salute to the autumn of human life.

Dictates of the democracy of death

1. Death belongs to life as birth does. It is a natural function, physiological in its working, and governed by the herd, being as egalitarian as disease. It is a herd function that finds expression at the level of an individual.

2. Death is essentially transcausal, transpathological. The medical obsession with the cause of death apparent only in hindsight, is an illusion that has been kept alive posthumously by modern medicine's success in passing ignorance off as knowledge.

3. Death is pantrajectorial for any species. As a herd function, the time of death is distributed over a wide range – from a very short to a very long life. The longer-lived owe a debt to the shorter-lived, as a part of their reciprocal responsibility. There is more than meets the eye in John Donne's 'Any man's death diminishes me'. *Ontolysis* i.e., one's own death, is but a gradual herd-lysis.

4. Death's dominance as a pantrajectorial force makes it an ever-present, and immediate reality, for the healthy as for the diseased, for the young as for the old. Death comes without warning and exercises its task peremptorily. This is reflected in an anonymous saying: 'Don't hope to repent at the eleventh hour; you may die at ten thirty.' Camus has put tellingly in *The Fall*: 'Don't wait for the last Judgment. It takes place every day.' In *Uttar Ramcharit,* an Indian Epic, the plea is pithy: *What you would want to do at the last moment, do it now.*

There is a positive side to the above, If death is here and now, so is life. Therefore any God-given moment is the right moment for the joy of living, the joy of loving, and the joy of being.

5. The climactic moment of death in its magnificence and munificence is beyond good and evil. Any natural death can be impartially and democratically a crowning glory.

DEATH

Implications for Modern Medicine

1. Thomas Jefferson inspired us with the adage that all men are created equal; they are endowed by their creator with certain 'unmedicable' rights; amongst these are developing, diseasing, and dying.

2. The serene nonchalance with which disease and death have treated modern medicine urges the medical technocrat all the more to be a compassionate friend. The fact that doctors cannot get to the cause of disease or death, nor alter their course should encourage medical personnel to regard no dis-ease, disease or even death as 'uncareable'.

The fact that *causation* of a disease in an individual is a herd function proscribes medical men from hurling an accusation at a patient for the latter's cancer or coronary, hypertension or hyperacidity, diabetes or deformity.

3. Because most cultures fear dying, one way to combat that dread is to look around for a scapegoat. Doctors see disease as *the* enemy and wreak vengeance on it. No wonder, the patient, the human being, is so easily lost sight of. The disease charts its adamant course; death keeps its own time. The treatment treats the doctor: a stage comes in many a terminal illness when the doctor treats *himself* by administering chemotherapy, radiation, a bypass, or a transplant to the patient. If only modern medicine were to care more, and 'cure' less!

> Thou shalt not kill
> But need'st not strive
> Officiously
> To keep alive.
> *Arthur Hugh Clough*

4. It is not for any small reason that most societies that function with less sophistication than the affluent West have better insight into the needs of the dying and their family. 'In the picture known to most physicians, the kindly, bearded humanitarian sits quietly by the bedside waiting for his little patient to die or recover: the

THE DICTATES OF THE NATURE OF DISEASE AND DEATH

decision is not his. There is hidden ignorance and sentimentality in the picture, but there is paradoxically great strength, beauty and spiritual dignity implicit in the situation portrayed. Much of this is denied today to members of the healing profession.' It is high time the medical man regains this majesty for himself and the bliss for his dying patient.

5. A good doctor may be defined as one 'who knows that he knows not.' In all humility, he ought to admit all the aspects of this *not knowing* as well as *knowing* to his patients, erasing thereby the needless dividing lines between the treater and the treated. Rutstein wrote in 1967 that, 'The public has been oversold. Even the most staid and accurate newspapers carry front-page reports on breakthroughs in the control of major illnesses at regular intervals. Thus, responsible publications cure cancer almost every week.' The iatrogenic illusion of the power to cure all makes people hope against hope to believe that death, not the doctor, would be the one to make an error. It is for the doctor to protect his patients from falling prey to such blind optimism.

6. Indian scriptures have classified the problems that the human frame is prone to, into two broad groups – (a) *gera* (akin to Gk. *geras* = old age) or time-governed senescence, and (b) *vyadhi* or disease because of, or independent of, the former. *Gera* or ageing is built into one's developmental programme, being innate, inevitable, and a mere function of the temporal flow. *Vyadhi* or disease when independent of *gera* is something one invites, a situation wrought upon oneself as a result of intemperance, irregularity, an indifference towards the body's *dharma*. *Gera* and death are inevitable; *vyadhi* is not. Many a person carries on through a long life without any disease or *vyadhi*.

The doctor is not capable of making an iota of difference in the working of *gera*; the doctor may be able to mitigate *vyadhi*. *Gera* as a function of time is as unfathomable as time itself. The summary failure of modern medicine to understand the cause, course, or the 'cure' of all age-related processes provides a scientific vindication of the scriptural insights.

DEATH

7. Medical men have an incurable penchant for holding meetings, seminars, conferences, workshops and congresses on a regional, national, continental, and global basis more than once in 365 days. The astutely advertised proceedings of such meetings create, in minds medical and lay, an illusion of medicine's relentless progress that reaches the public as decorously printed *Modern Trends, Recent Advances, Clinical Progress,* and so on. The rich payoff has been a matter of envy even for Madison Avenue: patients get seduced into the medical whirlpool; governments and international funding agencies enthusiastically pour more money in the pious belief that the more you spend, the better everyone feels. The incomparable cost spiral exhibited by the 'health industry' in developing countries is a direct outcome of medicine's inability to see, speak, and communicate the realities that surround human diseasing and death.

8. A global survey of the medical scene reveals that 9 out of 10 pills, potions, or procedures that are prescribed to patients are unnecessary, if not harmful. As often as patients get well because of the doctors, or worse for the same reason, do they get better despite the doctor. This chastizing data drives home two guiding lessons for medical men – firstly, of the wisdom of omission epitomised in the Hippocratic *primum non nocere* which means above all (do) no harm, and secondly, of the humility that must govern every act of commission, best stated over 400 years ago by Ambroise Pare, the father of French surgery: *Je le pensay, et Dieu le guarit,* which means I dressed him, and God healed him.

9. The above must make it clear that the essential relationship between a physician and his patient is one of *faith* – the former thinks he can cure, the latter feels he can be cured. Down-to-earth humanism demands, that, at least in matters of health and disease, dying and death, faith is a phenomenon that should not be exploited by the 'powerful' medical men, makers of drugs/instruments, hospitals and research institutes at the inevitable expense of the 'powerless' patients.

THE DICTATES OF THE NATURE OF DISEASE AND DEATH

10. A venerated general practitioner of Bandra, Bombay, has left a laudable legacy for medical men: Dr. Vaidya urged that any system of medicine – allopathy, homeopathy, naturopathy, etc. – is good for the patients provided it is mixed with adequate doses of sympathy and empathy.

Thanatognosis: Doctors and the dying

> It has been noted that the doctor is less mysterious and less absolute in the home than he is in the hospital. This is because in the hospital he is a part of a bureaucracy whose power depends on discipline, organization, and anonymity. These hospital conditions have given rise to a new model of medicalized death.
>
> Death has ceased to be accepted as a natural, necessary phenomenon. Death is a failure, a business lost. This is the attitude of the doctor, who claims the control of death as his mission in life. But the doctor is merely a spokesman for society. When death arrives, it is regarded as an accident, a sign of helplessness or clumsiness that must be put out of mind.
>
> Phillippe Ariés

The picture drawn by Ariés – all too common in the hospital and in the home in the developed countries, and becoming common in developing countries such as India – is a paralyzing side-effect of medical treatment that is too trustful of technique, too ignorant of death and the realities of disease and dying.

It is for the medical man to redress this imbalance. The doctor, for whatever reasons, has turned into the most important intermediary between a patient's disease and his dissolution, the final arbiter of how the patient, and his dear ones will conduct themselves when death seems near. The doctor must teach the art of 'learning to die' – the final lesson, that few doctors know how to impart, by preaching or by precept. Towards this imperative, set below are some helpful and practicable generalizations for the medical art of thanatognosis.

DEATH

1. The physicianly art of knowing about a patient's 'death in prospect' and acting accordingly for the welfare of the patient and his family can be called *thanatognosis,* comparable etymologically and professionally, to diagnosis. If the 'gnostic' part of diagnosis and prognosis guides a doctor in the management of a patient's illness, the 'gnostic' part of the art of thanatognosis helps the doctor, and through him the patient and the family, to face death realistically, courageously, and in good cheer.

Strange as it may seem, the readiness of the doctor to learn and exercise the thanatognostic art can be soothing treatment for the doctor himself by freeing him from the guilt and anxiety often associated with his inability to prolong his patient's life. The doctor could take consolation from Murchie's version of the Sixth Commandment: 'Thou shalt not kill – neither shalt thou obstruct a healthy or needful death.'

2. Along the course of a patient's illness, the doctor should – at an appropriate time determined by the nature of illness and its response to various therapies – realize that there is 'nothing else to be done'. At this stage, the physician stops treating the disease and starts guiding the patient and his relations towards a more enlightened outlook on death.

3. The patient and the people around should be taken into confidence and be made to participate in accepting the nearness of death. Compassionate discussions can make the patient and the family consider death as a real possibility, a meaningful desensitization that is achieved gradually and to begin with, painfully. The discussions should not have an aura of sorrow. As Kübler-Ross, pioneer thanatologist has stated, 'It might be helpful if more people would talk about death and dying as an intrinsic part of life just as they do not hesitate to mention when someone is expecting a new baby.'

4. Predicting exactly the time of death is impossible. Death will come sooner or later. Driving home to a patient and the family that another 'normal' human being may die of the same disease much earlier than the patient can go a long way towards easing their sense of being victimized.

THE DICTATES OF THE NATURE OF DISEASE AND DEATH

5. The dissociation between the presumed 'lethal' or 'terminal' illness and resultant death must be spelled out through personally known examples, through lay or medical literature, and through the realization that death by itself is a pristine physiological function that uses health and disease alike to suit its purpose. The patient must therefore be told that any disease can be comfortably and creatively lived with. Freud lived for 17 years with his cancer, Pasteur with his stroke for 27 years, and Solzhenitsyn has already lived with his cancer for over 25 years. The seemingly grim reality of 'death-here-and-now' the patient must be taught, is as much for those in full health, as for those beset with disease. The motto therefore ought to be while we are living, let us *live*, here and now to our fullest.

6. The patient and the family should be led into appreciating that dying with dignity is an honourable duty which, when well-performed, can permit the one who dies and those who survive him to tell death to "be not proud." Dying with dignity is dying victorious over death.

7. Thanatognosis should not be reserved only for the moribund patients. Patients 'terminally ill' and fit for thanatognosis should mean those for whom nothing further is to be done therapeutically, but who are otherwise fully alive to their surroundings, to the people around them and to their own self. (While administering specific therapies to the patient, the therapist should not compromise with this right to be alive). Thanatognostic advice from a doctor is something that the patient should comprehend, and accept, while in full possesion of his senses.

8. Kübler-Ross once wrote, 'Guilt is perhaps the most painful companion of death.' Therapeutic crusaders and preventionists, with their 'do-gooder' tirade against the killers of men, breed remorse and guilt to a pernicious degree in patients and their relations. The guilt centers around having smoked, having neglected the symptoms, not having taken the *right* kind of treatment, not having sufficiently suckled one's children thus ending up with, say, breast cancer, and so on. The art of

thanatognosis must strive at freedom from this burden of guilt. The doctor should explain that there are innumerable patients suffering from cancer, heart disease and diabetes despite their ascetic and temperate lives, that early treatment can mean early death, that neglect of symptoms does not unfavorably alter the course of the disease, and so on.

9. The awareness of the proximity of death raises a question in the mind of the patient: do the life spent and the small ration of it now left have, have they ever had, any meaning? Mustering all his compassion and competence, it is for the doctor to assure the patient that what was, what is, and what shall be is *right*. Putting it in the terminology of Victor Frankl, it is for the doctor to administer to the patient a dose, and an adequate one at that, of the meaningfulness of the patient's life, and of the patient's dying and death. Intensity of life and the fullness of being are not functions of temporal duration, for 'we all are but a moment's sunlight.'

10. The worst complex gnawing at a patient with a statistically determined disease such as cancer or heart attack is, of course the resentful 'why me?' A patient who had committed a cancerogenic blunder may guiltily reconcile himself to his having cancer, but what about the many who not having made any such incriminatable slip, develop cancer? 'Don't come and tell me this is God's will for me,' is a cry which typifies the desperate indignation of a dying person which can only be assuaged by making people at large understand that this is the will of God for one and all, and that staggered mortality is planned herd-lysis, with some dying of something at 9 years and some at 19 or 90 of the same thing or something else. The resolving of such questions as 'Why me?' or 'why *my* dear one?' may be the most difficult task for the doctor, and his success would greatly depend on how enlightened and how realistic about death the humans he is handling are.

11. The dying patient and, more than he, the family, are ready to spend any amount to get the 'right' treatment or cure for the patient. This explains many of the international safaris under-

THE DICTATES OF THE NATURE OF DISEASE AND DEATH

taken in search of more modern treatment. The customer's readiness to spend is inordinately boosted by the medically floated myth that, with the right amount of money and the right equipment, any disease can be successfully combatted. It is the duty of the doctor exercising thanatognosis to put an end to such illusions so that those who survive the dead are not reduced to penury and debt.

12. While thanatognosing, the most important pill, potion or procedure to be administered to the patient is *the doctor's time;* a relaxed and unhurried interest evinced in a patient can beget an interaction that eases the patient and educates the physician. If the patient is in any mental and/or physical distress, all palliative measures should be judiciously employed towards easing the discomfort of the patient.

13. Put briefly, the art of thanatognosing aims at making the patient *live* until he dies, well and with dignity. It also means guarding the patient against censure by family, society, and other medical men.

The payoff from thanatognosis, as an important branch of medical practice, can be quite satisfying for the doctor, quite blissful for the patient, and quite consoling for the patients's family. If dying is the final act that the (really) living must perform, then the act ought to be an artistic one. Talking in theatrical terms, if the final act is a piece of art, the patient dies an artist; if the act is a dragging flop, he dies a failure, an outcast. Which patient-artist and which doctor-director would abjure this golden opportunity of making the final bow an artistic one?

The Indian scriptures have it that an average person comes to know three days in advance the time of his death. Ariés has described how, in Europe, until the advent of the medicalization of death, a timely premonition of one's death was every man's prerogative – a timely warning that was greeted naturally and spontaneously. The trustworthy wisdom of ordinary people had it that no death, even from an accident or following too great an emotional shock, was or could be sudden. And if it did come suddenly, that is without the advance warning, it was called *mors repentina,* being ignominous, shameful, and an act of God's wrath.

The more death was medicalized, the more people grew insensitive to the act of dying and started seeing death as, at worst, an avoidable evil. Present times could be described as the age of *mors repentina* for almost every one. Medical men ought to rekindle in themselves and their patients the innate ability in every human being to know of one's death in advance, and to accord it a spontaneous welcome, as was done in the past. That achieved, the thanatognostic task of the doctor would be eased tremendously. In fact, the onus and the honour of exercising it would shift onto the patient – the ultimate in self-care.

CHAPTER 8   Reverence for Death is Reverence for Life

> He realized now that to be afraid of this death he was staring at with animal terror meant to be afraid of life. Fear of dying justified a limitless attachment to what is alive in man. And all those who had not made the gestures necessary to live their lives, all those who feared and exalted impotence – they were afraid of death because of the sanction it gave to a life in which they had not been involved. They had not lived enough, never having lived at all.
>
> *Albert Camus*

They had not lived enough, never having lived at all. And those who can't live well, can't die well, for *dying* is the last act that the living perform. Life and death are not absolute experiences belonging to separate categories, but are just two sides of the same reality, the seemingly polar opposites that are but parts of a single, larger whole. A good death, a happy one at that, then, is a crowning glory to a good, happy life.

In *The Art of Loving,* Fromm distinguishes between the 'love of emotion' and the 'love of decision', the former by its very nature evanescent, the latter, abiding. An abiding love of life can spring only from a decision, a resolve to love life. And such a resolve, scriptures and seers, philosophers and writers emphasize, has as its underlying fountainhead, the acceptance of death.

Talking of terminal cases, Kübler-Ross has described 'the stage of acceptance'; a time when the patient comes to terms with the prospect of death, and makes peace with it. Should not all of us, even in health, weave this thread of the acceptance of death into the very fabric of our life? The fairest deaths, Montaigne declared, are those that are the most voluntary, to which

Fontaine added; 'Death never takes the wise man by surprise; He is always ready to go.'

Death in life

The eminent biologist and Nobel-laureate Jacob has concluded his tome *The Logic of Living Systems* by a generalization that precisely and intrinsically programmed death is inherent to every form of life. That life here and now is equivalent to death here and now, is the most scientific and the most profound truth about life and death. Such scientifically-based reverence for death and reverence for life leads us to deliberate upon *euthanasia* (good death) and *euvivasia (good life)*.

Euthanasia: a semantic error

The lexicographic error is to define *euthanasia* as 'mercy killing;' a classical example of the bad use of a good word. An editorial in *The Medical Journal of Australia* pointed out that by conventional standards and by the law as it is, euthanasia means murder: 'Behind this is the blunt fact that euthanasia, for all the mildness of its root meaning, in current usage means the active and deliberate ending of a life – that is killing.' A *British Medical Journal* editorial written in a similar vein concluded that what now connotes euthanasia had better be replaced by the concept of assisted suicide. The conundrum is traceable to the fact that, as a cover for our conceptual inadequacies, euthanasia has been forced to mean the monstrous hybrid called mercy-killing.

Huxley, in *The Perennial Philosophy*, has asserted that many a thought is unthinkable without appropriate vocabulary and a frame of reference. Let us use Huxley's statement to clear the seemingly insoluble confusion and to return to euthanasia its pristine benignity and glory. Towards this, we may also be helped by Apley who pointed out that we indispensably need new words to keep abreast of new ideas.

Eu- as a prefix clearly implies 'good' or 'well'; thus we have eupepsia, euphoria, eugenics and so on. Euthanasia then means good death, and not, as the *British Medical Journal* erroneously assumed, an 'easy death.' What the so-called euthanasia or mercy-killing purports to provide is a swift end to the process of dying, a quick death that could logically be called *tachythanasia (tachy* meaning 'quick' or 'rapid'). When Sigmund Freud suffering at 83 from an obstinate oral carcinoma for 17 years was injected with four centigrams of morphine by his physician-friend Max Schur, he was not euthanatized, but tachythanatized. Tachythanasia could be defined as a medically-eased-death.

The distinction between euthanasia and tachythanasia is in order: euthanasia is self-earned, self-willed dignified departure unsullied by any medical intervention or condescension. Tachythanasia is a medically offered facility that helps to expedite the task a patient is already engaged in – protracted dying. It should be clear that tachythanasia is not assisted suicide. Jumping into the Thames or off the Eiffel Tower also is not tachythanasia. It is suicide. Dysthanasia, a bad death, on the other hand is, in the opinion of many, a common sin of modern medicine. Medical technology has made dying lonely, gruesome, dehumanised, mechanical, obscene and immensely troublesome. The fact that modern medicine has chosen to distort euthanasia to suit itself, and has not bothered to label as dysthanasia much that it does, speaks of the current intellectual crisis in medical thinking.

It is a paradox of modern times that medical men are busy prolonging the lives of diseased, senescent individuals, while destroying, quite lawfully, nascent fully-formed fetuses. It is equally paradoxical that the Japanese, who pioneered the free abortion movement soon after the Second World War, should have recently prosecuted and punished a helpless father who felt compelled to put an end to the life of his desperately handicapped son. Sir Theodore Fox, lately the editor of *The Lancet*, has declared that 'Life is not the most important thing in life.' If heart attack, stroke or cancer takes away a human being in a split second by engendering what may be called a 'guillotine-death,' then each of these very diseases, as a necessary polar-opposite, makes itself a protracted affair, where in the soul of the patient is a suffering prisoner of the ailing soma.

DEATH

Euvivasia: A good life a means to a good death

The balancing opposite of, and the highway to, euthanasia is euvivasia – a good life, a yea-saying to life that ends with a yea-saying to death. Describing euvivasia is too tall an order, but an attempt may be made by weaving the theme around Schweitzer's concept – reverence for life. The meaning of existence is to preserve unspoiled, undisturbed and undistorted the image of eternity with which each person is born. A genuine sense of reverence for the elements within and around us, can help each one of us steer our life towards imparting to our existence a meaning, towards living a good life culminating in a good death.

Reverence for time

The only representative of the eternal time that the mortal being has control over and access to is *this moment*, a realization that springs not from a business executive's utilitarian regard for time, but a homage to *This Timeless Moment*. The disease of modern times is hastiness and superficiality, a pathology rooted in man's inability and reluctance to revere each moment as an inseparable part of eternity.

The overcrowded curricula and the shallow media foster the obsession of time only as a means to lucre, laurels or levity. In the absence of such gains, the best that people can do is to *kill time*. Time only for gain compels the adoption of haste and superficiality, and these in turn, spawn a perpetual chase for the new. 'What's new?' is an interesting and broadening eternal question, but one which, if pursued exclusively, as is the raging fashion, results more often than not in an endless parade of trivia, the silt of tomorrow, and the fossil of the day after.

Should not this acquisitive, overachieving, information-obsessed, technological society call a halt to its progress, and declare the worth of the idea of beholding Heaven in a wild flower, and infinity in the palm of one's hand? In *Janus*, Koestler points out the striking disparity between the growth-curves of science and technology on the one hand, and of ethical conduct on the other, as evidenced by the sixth century B.C. emergence of

REVERENCE FOR DEATH IS REVERENCE FOR LIFE

Taoism, Confucianism and Buddhism, and the twentieth century burdens of Stalinism, Hitlerism and Maoism. In *Candle in the Wind*, Solzhenitsyn, through Alex and his urbanized uncle, debates the gains of electricity versus *no* electricity: 'Did Plato have a battery? Did Mozart have 220 volts? In candlelight, Uncle, your heart opens up.' In the face of death, there is no escape from allowing the inner light to illuminate our hearts, our lives, our every *this moment*.

Reverence for self

'Oh my dear, you are one in a million.' This affectionate assurance from a grandmother can with impunity be multiplied 4000 times to declare that each one of us is one in 4 billion. Outside a Yoga Center in Bombay is written: 'Each living being is a new thought of God.' The atheist could take this God as the bioforce of a Generator, Operator, Destroyer, or as a Gene Ordered Design. Be it as it may, each one of us has the blessing, the privilege of being a unique person, the like of which is not to be found now, nor in the past, nor in the future. Let each one of us be proud of this uniqueness.

The world is waking up to the innate wisdom of the scriptures. It is a pity that the utilitarian, demeaning educational systems the world over, floundering in the quagmire of comparative evaluations of human beings, unregenerately succeed in smothering the awesome truth of each person's right to exist. This truth lost, most of us die a thousand deaths every day till bodily death puts an end to this dying. Suicide is a crude expression of such self-denial. In Japan, for example, the approach of spring traditionally brings a countrywide suicidal rush; a major factor in this phenomenon is that school examination results are made known by April and the victims of Japan's competitive educational system often kill themselves rather than carry the stigma of failure throughout their lives. Every year, hundreds of children in Japan commit suicide after learning that they have disgraced themselves in exams. What price progress! This example, widely found in the West and likely to infect the developing East, is a strong incentive towards reviving some eternal values whereby human beings are taught, from the very start of life, to value their own self as larger, grander and more important than marks, grades, position, possessions, or shared opinions.

Solzhenitsyn once wrote, 'It is enough if you don't freeze in the cold and if thirst and hunger don't claw at your insides, if your back isn't broken, if your feet can walk, if both arms can bend, if your eyes see, and if both your ears hear, then whom should you envy? And why?' Each one of us, as a rightful individual in the universe, owns the moon and the stars, each one of us is cosmically rich. Rachel Carson, the author of *Silent Spring* drives home the importance of *a sense of wonder* as one of the requisites for full living. The much acclaimed seven wonders of the world will go down in history as the greatest understatements of all times: what is it that is not wonderful? The *Zen* Masters advise seeing life's every moment, every little act with the 'everyday mind' whereby life – routine, humdrum life – becomes not only a way to enlightenment but enlightenment itself. In *Zen*, one who has achieved *satori* (enlightenment), lives entirely in the present, gives fullest attention to everyday affairs, and experiences unceasingly the wonders and mysteries of life in every little act:

> How wonderous this, how mysterious!
> I carry fuel, I draw water.
> I can wonder, I can see.
> I can hear the music of the spheres.

Countering this conception is the indifference, the neglect, the injustice that the modern human being perpetrates on his or her own self in the name of being successful and sociable. The two wheels on which the chariot of sound health runs are proper sleep and proper food, towards achieving which the body sends out, day in and day out, a thousand signals and silent pleas in consonance with one's individuality. To suit the conviviality of a party, to meet a deadline, to please a business contact, nourishment gets perverted, sleep abjured and distorted. The climax is reached when a person must take a pill to sleep and a pill to keep awake. Lin Yutang has defined happiness as largely a matter of good digestion, while Sophocles defined it as the only medicine that gives ease. The science of Yoga teaches, as a primary requirement, the ability to sleep soundly and refreshingly.

Medicine, which boasts of knowing how many nanograms (a nanogram is a 1000 millionth of a gram) of a vitamin are needed by the human body, might be better employed to research into how much of right thinking and right living – even prayer, meditation, compassion – are needed to make for a better person, a better life.

Reverence for the living

The *grand unity of life* manifests itself through the intriguing genetic, structural and functional similarities exhibited by all living forms, from plankton and protozoa to the primates, and plants. Life implores and deserves reverence.

'Oreshchenkov offered him the cake as an equal, and he took it as an equal.' The 'he' there was intelligent, sad-eyed, tranquil, thoughtful, even transcendental – and 'he' was a dog. Joy Adamson could grow eloquent the same way for a lioness, Schaller for a gorilla or an Indian mahout for an elephant. Dhoomketu, a noted Gujarati writer, has described the true-life story of Ali and his buffalo; the latter caught inextricably in a train-track, sees to it that his master Ali who was trying to save the animal, is thrown to safety before the train runs the animal over. Nobility, lofty and poignant, is far from an exclusive human feature. *The Secret Life of Plants* has awakened us to the glory of the botanical kingdom, and the rapidly advancing deserts and the recurrent famines have driven home to us the link that human life has with trees – probably the sole example of life with *all goods* and *no bads*. Jainism ordains that hurting a leaf or a petal is tantamount to violating the divine order. There is an old Chinese saying: 'If you cut a blade of grass, you shake the universe.'

Everything that throbs with life is an integral and interconnected part of the universe. Plant and animal life may be sacrificed to meet human necessities, but not luxuries. The butchering of magnificent whales for cosmetics and the clubbing to death of seal-pups for fur coats represent man's tyranny over other fellow life forms at it worst; a bestiality that demeans human life.

If plants and animals must be respected, what of man? Avaricious and fiercely competitive modern living has robbed mankind of the faculty of seeing another human being as a fellow child of the universe. Human beings, in countries rich and poor, are often weighed on the scale of utility, as a means to an end, with results that have been a chronic despair for philosophers. Schweitzer has summed up the problem and its solution in his characteristic way: 'Wherever there is lost the consciousness that every man is an object of concern for us just because he is a man, civilization and morals are shaken, and the advance to fully developed inhumanity is only a question of time.'

This elaboration on the 'doctrine of divinity dwelling in all living creatures' is no attempt at preaching, but a pointer towards achieving *euvivasia*, or good life. Some moral values are essential for human life; one such important value is reverence for life, reverence for all that is living.

Reverence for the dying

The *dying* are persons – not always in need of one more investigation or operation, but a kind word, an affectionate squeeze, a warm pep talk; in short, love. The recent Hospice movement owes its origin, in part, to the realization that doctors treating terminal cases are frequently too obsessed with the disease process and have too little concern for the patient as a person. 'Today', according to an article 'A Good Death' in *Newsweek*, 'when mistakenly prolonged attempts at cures are at last abandoned, many doctors desert the dying, who are left unsupported at the most demanding point of their illness.' The kith and kin of the dying, with their overweening regard for medical men and nursing homes, follow the doctors and give up the dying when they most need the human touch, or a plain, humane 'hello'.

What relevance do the dying have to a good life? It is multifold. Each dying person is a model of what is inevitably going to befall another person. What is more important, it is one's witnessing or assisting good, dignified dying that prepares oneself for the event; perhaps a utilitarian, selfish viewpoint, but a valid one.

Beyond one's selfishness, there is the altruistic challenge, of making somebody's moment of dying, the moment of soul-satisfying living. The dying can't do much, but they can feel a lot. The dying cannot hurt, only love, and be loved. The dying being close to us, offer us the last, parting chance to grow up, to understand them, to love them.

The Hospice Movement could be defined as institutionalized reverence for the dying. It has been rightly described as a therapeutic community within a society, helping the living to live until they die. The Hospice movement must, in spirit, move into every home whereby the survivors learn to help dignify the passage of the dying by giving and thus receiving. George Eliot's assurance that 'the growing good of the world is partly dependent on unhistoric acts' allows the near-ones of the dying to love and console the latter, without much effort, expense, or medical intervention. The dying are worthy of reverence, for they are the best teachers that we have.

Euthanasia: A good death

Euthanasia is climactic to *euvivasia*. It is difficult to spell out its method. Humble inquiries into the lives of people around would reveal for oneself the true death-story of many who died a good death, without any medical tutoring. They could predict their end and welcome it, as they would a friend. Some could even time it. Robert Platt, the English physician and writer, relates the case of a vivacious young Scandinavian with progressive pulmonary fibrosis, admitted to an English hospital during the Second World War. One day he asked a nurse what hour would a patient's death cause the least bother to others. Next day, he was found dead, at the time he was apprised of. A celebrated example, of yet a younger person, is of John Gunther Jr., who, in the words of his father, died without any fear or pain. We personally witnessed, recently, a robust, lively man of 88 suddenly discovering that he had throat cancer. He said, 'My time is up.' For 3 months thereafter, until his death following a heart attack, he was a picture of grace, gratitude and what is more, love and affection.

Amongst the deaths of the notables, two are worthy of mention here – Haldane, and Einstein. JBS Haldane had cancer of the rectum, and typical of him, he died after leaving behind an elegaic tribute to his own cancer. 'Cancer' he wrote, 'can be rather fun/Provided one confronts the tumour/With a sufficient sense of humour.' Of his death from it, he admitted that 'I know cancer often kills/But so do cars and sleeping pills.' Einstein's final hours have been described by his daughter Margot: 'I did not recognize him at first – so changed was he by the pain and the lack of blood in his face. But his manner was the same. He was glad that I was looking a little better, joked with me and faced his own state with complete superiority; he talked with perfect calm, even with slight humour about the doctors, and was waiting for his end as if for an expected "natural phenomenon". As fearless as he was in life, so quietly and modestly he faced his death. He left this world without sentimentality and without regret.'

There are some gifted individuals who know the time of their death, a kind of personal thanatognosis. An example close to the authors is cited here. Mrs. K, who died at the age of 80, predicted her death 16 months earlier at a time when she was enjoying full health. On the appointed day –Narsinhachaudash, a holy day amongst Hindus – all her family members came and took her blessings. Her doctor-son checked her in the evening and assured everyone that she was perfectly normal. A little later, she requested that she be left alone. She prayed, and died soon after. A veterinary surgeon of Bombay has described the *willed death* of a dog under poignant circumstances. A dog was run over by a car that left him severely injured, paraplegic and in shock. Admitted to the hospital, the doctors said that he would not survive for more than a few hours. The dog's master was in

REVERENCE FOR DEATH IS REVERENCE FOR LIFE

England, and his return to Bombay took three days. The dog lingered on. The master rushed from the airport to the hospital. He took the dog's head in his lap, and while he was stroking his head, the dog passed away.

Reverence for life is Schweitzer's legacy to mankind which deserves a balancing opposite, a reverence for death. This dual concept in its manifold sense, is a way towards still farther reaches of human nature, and human soul. It is good, for man, to revere death so that he can revere life.

CHAPTER 9 Life and Death: Here and Now

> Nowness is with us, of us but yet always elusively evading our grasp. Bringing ourselves into the here and now sounds deceptively simple but is essentially very difficult. We divide life into a series of events and happenings which are seen as big and small. We mainly live our lives by concentrating on those events and people seen as large and important. Living becomes a series of time holes punctuated by occasional big happenings.
>
> David Brandon

The recent human past, largely dominated by the West, has been a veritable, scientific experiment: the whole project started off with the idea – which still persists – that once nature is subdued, hunger abolished and human beings provided with comforts, gadgets, and conveniences the *ennui* of existence would disappear, and happiness, a sense of meaning will be the lot of mankind. Alas, the experiment continues, but its results are far from encouraging: leading Western humanists – Schweitzer, Carrell, Jung, Frankl, Fromm, Koestler – have concluded that mankind, by all its misdeeds, has more than vindicated Shakespeare's lamentation:

> Man, proud man,
> Drest in a little brief authority,
> Most ignorant of what he's most assured,
> His glassy essence, like an angry ape,
> Plays such a fantastic tricks before high heaven
> As make the angels weep.

And if the angels are weeping, mankind has no hopes for any

redemption, any meaning, any sense of worthwhileness, of the trajectory of its life, signalled by an unwilled birth and ended by an inevitable death.

Materially prosperous, man is still poor and miserable, reminding us of the man portrayed by John Bunyan in the very first paragraph of *The Pilgrim's Progress* – a man clothed in rags (of nylon and rayon), (an ad-man's) book in his hand, a great burden (of things) upon his back, and as he reads, he weeps and trembles, and not being able to contain himself, he breaks out with the cry, 'What shall I do?'

What indeed? Were material things the highway to human happiness most of the haves would be happy and blissful by now. Paradoxically, the more things a man has, the more miserable he becomes. The universality of this predicament of man is symptomatic both of man's unexpressed and unheard plea to get himself out of this mess, and of man's happiness being rooted not in the joys of material goods but in those of the mind. Man is mind. It is no wonder that the human mind has been described as an instrument that can make heaven of hell, hell of heaven, can bind man forever or liberate him in but the twinkling of an eye.

Liberation? Yes. Why? That is man's essential lot. How? Through the mind. When? Here and now. How long? Forever, well beyond death. At what cost? None; in fact, the more liberated a man is, the richer he feels.

Modern man's Search for Meaning

> Man is made by his mind.
> As he thinks, so he is.
>
> The Bhagvad Gita
(The Song of the Blessed)

Man, mind, and *meaning* comprise a trinity in tandem. The term *man* is etymologically traceable both in Sanskrit and in English, to the Sanskrit root *manas* meaning *mind.* Therefore, man is that which has mind. Further, it is significant that both the terms *mind* and *meaning* are Indo-European gifts to mankind, derived

DEATH

from the root *men/menen* signifying thought, contemplation, consideration. Man is blessed (or cursed) with the desire to find meaning in everything, and above all, his own self.

A Helping hand from the West

The incredible sophistication with which modern science has revealed to us the complexity of biological organization from man to microbes has left us all gaping in amazement: each man, animal, cell, segment of DNA, on its own is like a marvel coded by a miracle enveloped in wonder, in an endless series fixed together liked a Russian doll. And yet – to give but one example of how far we all are from biological reality – it has been stated that to study a cell with the currently available gadgets including the electron microscopes, is like attempting to repair a delicate wrist watch with a sledge hammer. It should not therefore come as a surprise that two contemporary biophilosophers, Lewis Thomas, and Lyall Watson, have argued that the greatest discovery of the twentieth century is that of human ignorance: 'We seem in recent years,' Watson says, 'to have grown through the confident adolescence of science into a philosophic maturity, prepared not only to admit our ignorance, but to come to terms with the fact that there are some things we can never know.' Epistemologically, the human faculty of wonder is born out of some knowledge of the *what,* but an utter ignorance of the *how* and *why* of a phenomenon, be it the Pyramid of Cheops made of 2.3 million blocks of stone, or the DNA helix with its repertoire of possible structural arrangements – each capable of begetting a unique individual – bordering on 256 followed by 2.4 billion zeros. A person, writing 24 hours a day, would take 45 years just to write 256 followed by 2.4 billion zeros.

What the sense of wonder brings in its wake is the double gift of humility and reverence, an affective state that finds its expression in philosophy. Alfred North Whitehead, after a full academic career of 40 years as a mathematician in England, moved to Harvard to occupy the chair of philosophy. And he explained his personal evolution thus: 'Philosophy is the product

LIFE AND DEATH: HERE AND NOW

of wonder ... Philosophy begins in wonder. And at the end, when philosophic thought has done its best, the wonder remains.' Philosophy, the dictionaries assert, is *scientia scientiarum,* the science of all sciences. Today, modern physics bristles more with philosophy than with physics. A similar philosophic bent can be accorded to the physician's art of having to deal with human birth, life, ageing, diseasing, and death. A noumenal approach, going well beyond the phenomenal, is overdue in modern medicine.

Nosce te ipsum: Gnothi seauton: Know thyself

The process of knowing oneself resides in expanding one's mind well beyond the limits of space and time, birth, life and death. A constant *awareness* of one's inherent universality, eternality resolves all possible identity crises by making one's self as large and as orderly as the cosmos. Such a realization forms a panexistential panacea that carries one's self through the thick and thin of life. A glimpse of the Eastern insight into the art of knowing oneself is now in order.

Grand Eastern Generalizations

The Eastern sages, with the seeing eye of their inner minds have given mankind some universal, reassuring pronouncements:

1. *Om Isavasyam–Idam Sarvam
   yat-kimcha Jagatyam Jagat.*

   All this, whatsoever moves in this universe, including the universe – itself moving – is indwelt, pervaded, enveloped, clothed by the Lord.

2. *Om Purnamadah purnamidam
   purnat purnamudacyate
   purnasya purnamadaya
   purnamevavasisyate*

   Completeness is that, completeness is this

from completeness, completeness comes forth.
Completeness from completeness taken away
completeness to completeness added,
completeness alone remains.

3. *Om, Aham Brahmosmi* meaning 'I am Brahman.'

4. *Om, Tat Twam Asi* meaning 'Thou art that.'

And when asked to expand on what really is Brahman, the sages gave three words.

Sat – Chit – Ananda meaning 'Existence – Awareness – Bliss.'

Viewed from a philosophical angle, each of the above statements is a *synthetic judgement a priori,* being an inductible aphorism that stands verified through ages, reinforced in fact by the insight that modern science and technology have provided. Much as this entire book is an appeal to the logical, left-side of the human brain, this chapter too is an effort to place before the reader ratiocinative concepts and data adequate enough to drive home to each one of us, the grandeur of being alive.

Isavasyam – Idam Sarvam: God is in everything

The vedic concept of God is no anthropomorphic, anthropocentric image or idol but an all pervading eternal reality. Shankara, Spinoza and Einstein have talked of this impersonal God who is not concerned with the deeds and fate of man but who reveals himself in the harmony of all beings. Spinoza in his time was called an atheist. The present discussion does not deny any atheist the right to participate in the logical exchange of ideas.

The concept of God-in-everything is the basis of Schweitzer's reverence for life and Gandhi's reverence for a pencil stub. Reverence for life is proof against the all too common human cruelty against a fellow human being. It is a readiness to see that the human heart throb is no different from, or superior to, the heart throb of an animal awaiting death in an abattoir or in an experimental laboratory. It is the wisdom of thinking a thousand times before felling a tree, for, its chloroplasts and our mitochondria are similar and God-given. Gandhi's regard for the inanimate is pregnant with a sense of frugality that prevents needless exploitation of the Earth's scarce resources.

Beyond the altruistic regard for life and things, beyond oneself, the concept of God-in-everything is essential for curing a benumbing, desperate sense of alienation to which the modern human being is prone. A fellowship of being enriches oneself and cuts across all barriers of race, religion, caste, creed, ignorance or learnedness, riches or poverty, to bring home the perennial worth of *love* as *the* mode of being and becoming, be it a day, a sunset, a leaf, a person, a dog, or a stone. A Sufi poet, when denied by a Kazi the right to drink wine in a mosque for that is the abode of Allah, posed a peremptory puzzle: 'Oh Kazi, let me drink wine right here in the mosque or show me some place where Allah is not.'

Purnamadah Purnamidam: Completeness prevails

In today's world, each one of us is born an emperor and grows into and dies a beggar because of our misplaced sense of importance. Modern education puts emphasis on information and qualifications and not on discrimination. The quality of living is considered in terms of the size and the location of a sprawling villa and curios therein. The intensively consumeristic living makes man crave more and more, assuming the shape of an obsessive disease that only ends with death.

An Indian folk song declares: 'Beyond the basic needs of a loin cloth, and some bread, all else is crap.' Its essence is that a human being, like the birds and the bees, attains fulfillment the moment the physiological needs of the body are met with; all else is ornamental. Hence the meaning, the sense of completeness of every human life *is*, during waking hours, in sleep, in infancy, in old age, in the remote places, in the metropolis, as a president or as a peon, in health and in sickness. At birth, the cosmic completeness takes shape as a carnal being, which at death once again merges into the cosmic completeness. Completeness *is*.

Man, in ignorance or disregard of this inherent completeness and perfection that attends every life, every breath, commits a double fault: he spots imperfections that are not, and then he presumes that he has the wisdom, and moreover, the power to rectify them. Advanced physics today asserts the unswaying role of *superdeterminism* – things, events and people have been, are, and will be the way they have been predetermined to be, from the time of the Big Bang. Man has now and again the illusion of success, the pride of victory, but his cardinal role is that of a *witness*; he is a person gifted with – as Jiddu Krishnamurthi put it – the choiceless awareness in a pathless land.

How powerful is man? To cite but one example: A single breath, the prerogative of any human being, is not his doing. He expands his chest, but it is the air that rushes in through forces that are beyond his knowing. When the Nobel-laureate physicist Kapitza under Stalinist duress was unable to return to his mentor Rutherford in England, he wrote in a letter: 'After all, we are only small particles of floating matter in a stream we call fate. All that we can manage is to deflect our tracks slightly and keep afloat – the stream governs us.' If Peter Kapitza, could share such love of fate with the father of atomic fission, it would be no shame for an average or an extraordinary man to do so. The existential role of such an approach has been best summarised by Durant: 'Such a philosophy teaches us to say Yea to life, and even to death. It calms our fretted egos with its large perspective; it reconciles us to the limitations within which our purpose must be circumscribed. It may lead to resignation and an Orientally supine passivity; but it is also the indispensable basis of all wisdom and all strength.'

Om, Aham Brahmosmi: I am Brahman

The shaper of Einsteinian space-time into objects and beings is *information,* the attributes of which are no different from those of the Vedic Brahman. Thus, it is neither matter (occupying no space), nor energy (having no need to travel) but is all pervading, all encompassing, omniscient, omnipresent, and omnipotent. It is there irrespective of the material universe. It *is* there, before

LIFE AND DEATH: HERE AND NOW

even the Big Bang was. Awareness or *chit*, the highest attribute of human mind, is a representative of this information or Brahman. Believe it or not, each man, cell, organism is Brahman. When the human mind realizes this truth, it declares: *I am Brahman.* The mind is man's means to measurelessness, infinitude, eternity.

Such self-realization is the highway to a state of bliss, contentment, awareness, that passes all understanding. One's cancer becomes, not a curse by a curious twist of fate, but a self-begotten programme, one's own flesh and blood, a part of the Brahmanic blueprint, a story integral to the continuum that birth, life, disease and death must and do exhibit.

The supreme role that a sense of self-respect can play, for each one of us is at the time of death, and thereafter. *The Tibetan Book of the Dead* and Indian thought which is in agreement with it, have it that each human being, around the time of death, is bathed in a light – 'brighter than a thousand suns' as the *Gita* puts it – which gives a glimpse of one's true universal, eternal nature. Having been thus taken to the edge of the infinite, the human being is now given a choice: 'Ask and it shall be given.' Most human beings, because of the state of bondage, end up wishing this and that, and the cosmos obliges; the cycle of birth and death continues. But, on the other hand, if the realization *I am Brahman* has truly penetrated one's being, then one asks for nothing, for how can Brahman itself ask anything from Brahman? And that, the scriptures say, is the basis of *nirvana, moksha,* or eternal liberation.

If all this sounds too esoteric, there are also simpler consolations. While in the carnal frame, the realization or a glimpse of one's innate Brahmanic nature, allows one to brave the disease and welcome death, for death is but a carnal way to become Brahman disincarnate. Let friendly disease and death be. Man innately has no quarrel with either.

Om, Tat Twam Asi: That art thou

A logical corollary of *I am Brahman* is *he, she or it is Brahman* and therefore I am he, she, it or everything. In the kingdom of the

Lord, everything, everybody is of equal importance; an integral part and reflection of the greater whole.

Chandogya Upanishad relates a dialogue between Svetaketu and his father. Svetaketu asks of the father: 'What is that tree?' And the father declares affirmatively: 'That art thou. Thou art that.' Then, in a series of questions, Svetaketu inquires about the nature of a thought, a metal pot, a bird, a goat, a clod of earth, a pool of water, a waft of breeze, and the father himself. And to every question from the son, the father returns with only one refrain: *'Tat twam asi:* That art thou.' *Advaitism* (monism) means that all is one, one is all, one and all are but just the same manifest Brahman.

With the dawning of the truth that whatever and whatsoever there is, *is me*, any feeling of envy, jealousy, estrangement, superiority or inferiority is replaced by a sense of oneness, a joy of participation, a celebration of an awareness. Such a person, in the words of Plotinus, is one of those who 'see all things, not in process of becoming, but in Being, and see themselves in the other. Each being contains in itself the whole intelligible world. Therefore All is everywhere. Each is there All, and All is each. Man as he now is has ceased to be the All. But when he ceases to be an Individual, he raises himself again and penetrates the whole world.'

In an age dominated by the media, where celebrities are oversung, money-spinners turned into heroes, the seemingly lucky ones portrayed as the examples to be followed; discontent, selfishness, the pursuit of gain, become the guiding forces of day-to-day existence. The result is stress, ulcers, alcoholism, drug addiction, homicides and suicides – a satanic gallery of 'achievements' plaguing the affluent countries and threatening to overtake the others. The fundamental change that must come – as the leading philosophers have been wishing – is an unswaying sense of self-respect and contentment, extended with equal felicity to all fellow beings, thereby achieving the double distinction of loving oneself and one's neighbour as well. This done, a fellow being's achievement does not seem as one more stressful incentive towards keeping up with the Joneses, but seeing in a Mozart, a Maugham or a Carl Lewis an extension of one's own self, not to be envied, but a delight to be shared.

The Seven Deadly Sins are psychodynamically rooted in the wilful denial of *Tat twam asi*: pride, covetousness, anger and envy are a mere corollary of asserting or chasing one's imagined superiority in a human fraternity where, in fact, all are inherently equal. Lust, for power or pleasure, springs from an infringement of the reverence for life. Gluttony reflects the denial of a self-evident truth: food is life that has the humility and altruism to sustain another life; it is mankind's saviour and should be revered as such – not an object of exploitation but Brahman incarnate, to be deified, and for which thanks should always be given. The shipwrecked Robinson Crusoe had bags of gold coins and no food, till the discarded corn conversed with the soil of the island to fill it up with life giving, lush green food. The Indian scriptures have ordained that grace be said prior to eating for at that time Brahman is merging with Brahman.

The sin of sloth may be appreciated with some difficulty. Modern man, in order to support his life style, needs to remove every year, twenty tons of raw material per capita from the bowels of Mother Earth. This rapaciousness is rooted in our slothful tendency to take from Mother Earth without bothering to return at least equally if not more. The slothful *Homo sapiens* (!) in reality is overdemanding, a sin that seems the most deadly of all. The generosity with which Earth treats man has been poignantly expressed in the idea that the Earth tickled with a hoe, laughs with a harvest.

Man is a child of the Earth; in Sanskrit, he is called *Partha,* the son of *Prithvi* that is *The Good Earth.* The endowment of the mind also means however that he can attain the enlightenment of *Sat-Chit-Ananda.*

Sat-Chit-Ananda: Existence-awareness-bliss

The *Katha Upanishad* meditates on the problems of daily living, and comes to an exacting pronouncement: much as the sharp edge of a razor is difficult to pass over, the path to salvation from

DEATH

the ennui and degradation of human existence is hard. But, it adds, the price is, at all times, worth its while. Mind your mind, and your *sapientia* will ensure your *Existence* with a constant *Awareness* of *Bliss*, for that is the essence of the formless Brahman, as well as the formed human being. Know thyself: You are *Sat-Chit-Anand,* absolutely, meaningfully; in birth, life, disease, death, herebefore, hereafter, in the eternal here and now.

CHAPTER 10 Life and Death: Before and Beyond

> We are afraid of death, because we are afraid of the absolute cessation of our personality. Therefore, if we realize the Person as the ultimate reality which we know in everything that we know, we find our own personality in the bosom of the eternal.
>
> To realize with the heart and mind the divine being who dwells within us is to be assured of everlasting life.
>
> Rabindranath Tagore

Death, the borderline between being and non-being makes man wonder, what am I, where from, where to? Life, here and now, possibly extends this side of birth and that side of death presenting to man's mind the possibility of an uninterrupted threefold existence; Herenow, Hereafter, and even, Herebefore – a ceaseless state of Being both in space and time, in infinity and in eternity. Such a conceptual leap takes man into the cosmic arena, into the cosmic whole. To this yearning of man for an understanding of the yonder on either side of life, science – advanced science – is responding with an exhilarating affirmation.

Cosmic interrelatedness: Advaitic wholeness

Science's positivism is based on the fact that the boundaries dividing the past, the present, and the future have become blurred, and the entire universe, both in terms of time and space, appears as one uninterrupted whole.

The latest certitude *vis-a-vis* cosmic wholeness in terms of both space and time, stems from Bell's theorem which declares that there are no such things as separate parts or separate events. All the 'parts' and all the 'events' are interconnected in an intimate and immediate way previously claimed only by the mystics. *Ab initio* to *ad eternum,* the Big Bang to the ultimate Black Hole, the universe is one continuous whole.

With this cosmic comprehension of the universal interconnectedness of things and events, the Big Bang, the Black Hole and the Buddha assume an interconnectedness, a oneness. In the words of a Tantric Buddhist, Lama Anagarika Govinda, 'The Buddhist does not believe in an independent or separately existing external world, into whose dynamic forces he could insert himself. The external world and his inner world are for him only two sides of the same fabric, in which the threads of all forces and of their objects, are woven into an inseparable net of endless, mutually conditioned relations.' Particle physics echoes this statement by generalizing that 'Every particle consists of all other particles.' Each atom is, and, as it were, contains all the 10^{84} atoms that comprise the visible universe.

Lest it be felt that Bell's theorem and its corollaries have been hastily overexploited, the reader's attention can be drawn, first, to the Einsteinian *space-time continuum,* and secondly, to the not commonly recognized *life-time continuum,* the former by now axiomatic in physics, the latter the basis of the biological uniqueness of every individual.

Space-time continuum

There is no such thing as space *and* time, only space-time. Space-time flows perpetually to form a continuum, an uninterrupted, unfragmentable whole. The Eastern sages, talk of an infinite, timeless and yet dynamic present, of the existence of *this eternal now*. As Hui-neng, a Zen Patriarch, put it; 'The absolute tranquility is the present moment. Though it is at this moment, there is no limit to this moment, and herein is eternal delight.' In the spiritual world, Suzuki emphasizes, there are no such temporal distinctions as the past, present and future, for they have rolled themselves into a single moment, the present moment.

LIFE AND DEATH: BEFORE AND BEYOND

Life-time continuum

The nature of the life-time continuum is not difficult to grasp. It may be recalled that *life is configured time,* an interconnected focal point in the fathomless ocean of time. The incontrovertible nature of the interconnectedness is driven home by the unprecedented, unparalleled, and unrepeatable uniqueness of every individual human being, every life-form, from the time life began. When a human being, say M, is in the process of developing in the mother's womb, its first zygotic cell and all the cells thereafter must know, there and then, of all the life-forms that have been, that are, and that will be, so that the *uniqueness* of M remains asserted, unviolated and unduplicated. Surely the ways of our selves and our cells are of immeasurable knowledge.

How come our human, M, knows of another human being a thousand years before and yet another being a thousand years hence? If the necessary 'information' were to travel, then even at the speed of light, it would take 1000 years before the embryonic cells of M know what to do. In reality, they know exactly what to do, in *no* time. This means that whatever information – in fact, all the information backwards, sidewards and forwards – the cells need to know is there. Matter, life in general, and we humans are configured by information – the noumenal Brahman, governing as it does the triad of space, time and energy that are the raw material for the phenomenal universe christened in Indian scriptures as the *Lila*.

> There was something formless yet complete,
> That existed before heaven and earth,
> Without sound, without substance,
> Dependent on nothing, unchanging,
> All-pervading, unfailing.

This passage from the scriptures describes *Brahman* on the one hand, and, in modern physics 'information' on the other. Brahman is 'information,' rightly described in the Hindu scriptures as smaller than the smallest, vaster than the vastest. A mundane exemplification of this idea is not far to seek: there is more information on organic chemical synthesis packed into the head of a spermatozoon than in all the 200 volumes of *The Journal of Biological Chemistry*. Encoded within the 0.0000000000001 gm of DNA of every mammalian cell is the total history of life.

Salt doll in the cosmic ocean

We are now ready to understand the Indian metaphor of salt doll in the ocean. Let us suppose that the cosmos is the size of, and the nature of, the Pacific ocean, and that we are concerning ourselves with the human, M, that we just talked about. Guided by information that spells M-ness, at some stage some salt of the ocean aggregates to form M. Over an appointed period of time, M, gathering yet more salt – or yet more cells – grows, decays and finally dissolves to become one with the ocean.

Three truths are clear: before M took recognizable corporeal form, M-specific information was there in communication with the rest of the ocean. This was M's pre-existence. During the carnate phase, M was connected uninterruptedly to the entire ocean. In the post-carnate phase, M-ness was (and, is) a part of the ocean, very much there to guide another N-in-the-making, not to be like M. M is as eternal as eternity, as infinite as infinity. For M, as for anyone, life is finite, but eternal. Here, hereafter, herebefore, M *is*.

The Tao of being here

One's uniqueness is a phenomenon extraordinary in the sense that an individual is a focal point, *the* central point of the whole universe, infinity, eternity. 'In the heaven of Indra,' as Mahayana Buddhism states 'there is said to be a network of pearls, so arranged that if you look at one you see all others reflected in it.'

In the words of Plotinus each being contains in itself the entire intelligible world; therefore, All is everywhere, each is All, and All is each. Leibniz described the world as being made of fundamental units called 'monads', each of which mirrors the whole universe. Buddhism insists that this state of interpenetration – one being containing, reflecting all others by being at the center of all others – is not comprehensible intellectually, but is to be experienced by an enlightened mind in a state of meditation. This rare gift of encompassing the whole creation, the entire cosmos in one's individual self is epitomized in the illuminated Indian self-awareness: I am Brahman.

The Eternal Herebefore and Hereafter

> The life on this plane is only for a short time, but from the standpoint of eternal life we are never born and we are never going to die, because we are birthless, deathless, eternal, immortal, and also part and parcel of the infinite Spirit which is worshipped under different names among different races.
>
> *Swami Abhedananda*

Can intuition or science offer some help in presenting the haziest concepts of before-birth and after-death, pre-existence and immortality? We may start with Tagore's wisdom summing up the personality of man: despite the obvious fact of death, man asserts his immortality by that deeper unity, that ultimate mystery in him which, while occupying his present, overflows its banks called the past and the future, through his body and beyond his body, through his mind and beyond his mind. Tagore's insight can be backed by what Jesus said: 'Before Abraham was, I am.' Since each one of us is but a configuration of the eternal spirit, each one of us *is* before birth, and continues to be, after death. Science, enriched by wisdom, has started talking of the eternal herebefore and hereafter – in confident terms. Pre-existence explains the continuity of life into the past, and immortality explains the continuity of life into the future.

Life thus presents the possibility of being, really, an uninterrupted three-timensional affair. 'Never did I not exist, nor you, nor will any of us, ever hereafter cease to be, ' assures the *Gita*. This is simply because, the *Gita* explains, existence can never be non-existence, neither can non-existence ever become existence. And *you* the *Gita* generalizes, *cannot* be burnt by fire, dried up by air, wetted by water, killed by swords. You are in reality complete, bliss incarnate, being the immortal, indestructible *awareness* that has been, is, and will be a perennial witness to the cosmic play.

Lest it be felt that such thoughts on eternal life – forwards and backwards – is an Indian obsession it should be remembered that students of comparative religion as well as those of history find such ideas among Christians, Jews, Zoroastrians, Chinese, Scandinavians, Greeks and Egyptians, philosophers like Pythagoras, Plato and neoplatonists like Plotinus, and poets like Wordsworth, Tennyson, and Whitman.

When Crito asked, 'In what way shall we bury you, Socrates?' Socrates replied: 'In any way you like, but first you must catch me, the real *me*. Be of good cheer, my dear Crito, and say that you are burying my body only, and do with *that* whatever is usual and what you think best.' What is this unburiable Socratic *me*, that refuses to go to the grave with the body? In ordinary terms it is man's personality or mind. In esoteric terms, it is his or her soul-force. This soul-force has two choices before it. The most common is karma-guided rebirth and reincarnation, as a part of the perpetual cycle: 'Whatsoever desire is very strong during the lifetime, becomes predominant at the time of death, and that desire,' the *Gita* declares, 'moulds the creation of the subtle body of the individual.' The uncommon is the choiceless, nirvanic merger, oneness with the cosmos. The salt doll, as it were, becomes the cosmos.

Bibliography

Abhedananda, Swami: *Life Beyond Death.* Ramakrishna Vedanta Math, Calcutta, 1978.
Abhedananda, Swami: *The Mystery of Death.* Ramakrishna Vedanta Math, Calcutta, 1978.
Adler, C.S., Stanford, G. and Adler Sheila M. (eds.): *We are But a Moment's Sunlight.* Pocket Books, New York, 1976.
Ardrey, R.: *African Genesis.* Collins, London, 1971.
Aries, P.: *The Hour of Our Death.* Vintage Books, New York, 1981.
Behavior: Doctors of the death camps. *Time,* June 25, 1979, p.48.
Bergson, H.: *Creative Evolution.* Tr. Arthur Mitchell. Henry Holt, New York, 1911.
Bhave, V.: *Bhoomi Putra* (Baroda, India), 1969.
Bohm, D.: *Causality and Chance in Modern Physics,* Univ. of Pennsylvania Press, Philadelphia, 1957.
Boyd, W.: *A Text book of Pathology.* Eighth Edition. Lea & Febiger, Philadelphia, 1970.
Brown, L.: *The Twenty Ninth Day.* W.W. Norton & Co., New York, 1978.
Budge, E.A.W.: *The Egyptian Book of the Dead.* Dover Publications, New York, 1967.
Burnet, F.M.: *Immunological Surveillance.* Pergamon Press, Oxford, 1970.
Burnet, F.M.: *Genes, Dreams and Realities.* MTP, Bucks, 1971.
Carrel, A.: *Man, the Unknown.* McFadden Publications, New York, 1961.
Columbia Encyclopedia, The: 3rd Edition, Columbia Univ. Press, New York, 1968.
Comfort, A: *Ageing: The Biology of Senescence.* Routledge & Kegan Paul, London, 1964.
Cregan, E.T., Moertel, C.G., O'Fallon, Judith, R., Schutt, A.J., O'Connell, M.J., Rubin, J. and Frytak, S.: Failure of high-dose vitamin C (ascorbic acid) therapy to benefit patients with advanced cancer: A controlled trial. *New Eng. J. Med.,* 301: 687-690, 1979.
Dobzhansky, T.: Heredity. In, *Mankind Evolving.* Yale Univ. Press, New Haven and London, 1962, pp.23-50.

DEATH

Editorial: A private blind alley. *Lancet*, 1: 779-780, 1972.
Editorial: Life-in-Death. *New Engl. J. Med.*, 256: 760-761, 1957.
Evans-Wentz, W.Y.: *The Tibetan Book of the Dead*. Causeway Books, New York, 1973.
Fries, J.F.: Aging, natural death, and the compression of morbidity. *New Engl. J. Med.*, 303: 130-135, 1980.
Hayflick, L.: The cell biology of human aging. *New Engl. J. Med.*, 295: 1302-1308, 1976.
Huxley, A.: *The Perennial Philosophy*. Fontana Books, Collins, London, 1966.
Gompertz, B.: On the nature of the functions expressive of the human mortality and on a new mode of determining life contingencies. *Phil. Trans. Roy. Soc.* (London), Ser. A., 115: 513, 1825.
Jacob, F.: *The Logic of Living Systems*. Orient Longman, New Delhi, 1975.
Jaffe, B.M.: Foreword. In, *Vascular Diseases – current controversies*. (Ed. P.N. Sawyer and R.M. Stillman). Appleton-Century-Crofts, New York, 1981.
Jungk, R.: *Brighter Than a Thousand Suns*. Victor Gollancz, London, 1958, p.65.
Kassirer, J.P. and Pauker, S.G.: The toss-up. *New Engl. J. Med.*, 305: 1467-1469, 1981.
Kastenbaum, R.J.: *Death, Society, & Human Experience*. C.V. Mosby Company, Saint Louis, 1977.
Knowles, J.H.: The responsibility of the individual. In, *Doing Better and Feeling Worse: Health in the United States*. (ed. J.H. Knowles), W.W. Norton and Co., New York, 1977, pp.57-80.
Koestler, A.: *Janus: A Summing Up*. Pan Books Ltd., London, 1978.
Kothari, M.L. and Mehta, Lopa A.: Trans-science aspects of disease and death. *Persp. Biol. Med.*, 24: 658-666, 1981.
Kothari, M.L. and Mehta, Lopa, A.: The Trans-technique aspects of disease and death. *J. Post. Grad. Med.*, 29: 75-81, 1983.
Kübler-Ross, Elizabeth: *On Death and Dying*. Macmillan, London 1969.
Kübler-Ross, Elizabeth: *Death: The Final Stage of Growth*. Prentice-Hall, New Jersey, 1975.
Kurtzke, J.F.: *Epidemiology of Cerebrovascular Disease*. Springer-Verlag, Berlin, 1969.
Leading Article: An easy death. *Brit. Med. J.*, 1:704, 1975.
Leading Article: The problems of legalizing euthanasia – and the

BIBLIOGRAPHY

alternative. *Med. J. Aust.,* 2: 667-668, 1976.
Lipkin, M.: The CPC as anachronism. *New Eng. J. Med.,* 301: 1113-1114, 1979.
Malleson, A.: *Need Your Doctor Be So Useless?* George Allen & Unwin, London, 1973.
McKeown, T.: Human malformations: Introduction. *Brit. Med. Bull.,* 32: 1-3, 1976.
Moody, R.A., Jr.: *Life After Life.* Bantam Book, New York, 1977.
Murchie, G.: *The Seven Mysteries of Life: An Exploration in Science and Philosophy.* Rider/Hutchinson, London, 1979.
Nadkarni, V.C.: Is there life after death? *Illustrated Weekly of India,* May 6-12, 1979, pp.6-11.
Opie, L.H.: Long distance running and sudden death. *New Engl. J. Med.,* 293: 941-942, 1975.
Osis, K. and Haraldson, E.: *At the Hour of Death.* Avon, New York, 1977.
Phillips, D.Z.: *Death and Immortality.* Macmillan, London, 1970.
Pickering, G.: *High Blood Pressure.* Churchill, London, 1968.
Platt, R.: Reflections on aging and death. *Lancet,* 1: 1-6, 1963.
Plessner, H.: On the relation of time to death. In, *Man and Time.* (ed. J. Campbell). Pantheon Books, New York, 1957, pp. 233-263.
Portmann, A.: Time in the life of the organism. In, *Ibid.* pp. 308-323.
Radhakrishnan, S.: *The Bhagvadgita.* Blackie & Son (India) Ltd., Bombay, 1974.
Radhakrishnan, S.: *The Principal Upanishads.* George Allen & Unwin Ltd., London 1978.
Relman, A.S.: Are the case records obsolete? Two views. *New Engl. J. Med.,* 1112-1113, 1979.
Rosenblatt, R.: The quality of mercy killing. *Time,* August 26, 1985, p.52.
Rutstein, D.D.: *The Coming Revolution in Medicine.* M.I.T. Press, Cambridge, 1967.
Shneidman, E.S.: *Deaths of Man.* Penguin Books, Baltimore, 1973.
Simms, H.S.: Longevity studies in rats. I. Relation between lifespan and age of onset of specific lesions. In, *Pathology of Laboratory Rats and Mice.* (Ed. E. Cotchin and F.J.C. Roe). Blackwell, Oxford, 1967, pp. 733-748.
Van der Leeuw, G.: Primordial time and final time. In, *Man and Time.* (ed. J. Campbell). Pantheon Books, NewYork, 1957, pp. 324-350.

Watson, L.: *Lifetide: The Biology of the Unconscious.* Coronet Books, Hodder and Stoughton, London, 1980.
Weinberg. A.M.: Science and trans-science. *Minerva,* 10: 209-222, 1972.
Will, G.F.: A good death. *Newsweek,* January 16, 1978, p.5.
Zukav, G.: *The Dancing Wu Li Masters: An Overview of the New Physics.* Bantam Books, New York, 1979.
Zumoff, B., Hart, H. and Hellman, L.: Considerations of mortality in certain chronic diseases. *Ann Intern. Med.,* 64: 595-601, 1966.

Name Index

Abhedananda, Swami, 117
Abraham, 117
Acheson, Dean, 57, 59
Achilles, 44
Adamson, Joy, 97
Ardrey, Robert, 45, 55, 65
Ariès, Phillippe, 85, 89

Bhave, Vinoba, 59
Boyd, W., 68
Brandon, David, 102
Brezhnev, Leonid, 35, 59
Brown, Lester, 76
Browne, Sir Thomas, 30, 32
Buddha, 114
Bunyan, John, 103
Burnet, Macfarlane, 26, 56, 57, 66
Byron, Lord, 62

Camus, Albert, 81, 91
Carrell, A., 102
Carson, Rachel, 96
Clough, Arthur Hugh, 82
Comfort, A., 34
Cousins, Norman, 73
Cregan, E.T., 42
Crito, 118
Cromwell, Oliver, 62
Crusoe, Robinson, 111
Curie, Marie, 7

de Gaulle, Charles, 57, 59
Dobzhansky, T., 59
Donne, John, 74, 81

Editorial/article, in
  British Medical Journal, 92, 93
  Newsweek, 98
  The Lancet, 79, 93
  The Medical Journal of Australia, 92

The New England Journal of
  Medicine, 49, 58, 76
Einstein, Albert, 21, 56, 62, 100, 106, 108, 114
Eliot, George, 97
Encyclopaedia Britannica, The New, 18

Fontaine, 92
Fox, Theodore, 93
France, Anatole, 62
Frankl, Victor, 88, 102
Freud, Sigmund, 35, 36, 87, 93,
Fromm, Erich, 91, 102,
Fuller, Thomas, 78

Gandhi, 40, 53, 54, 106, 107
George, King the VI, 53, 54
Gompertz, B., 36, 76,
Graunt, 36
Gunther, John Jr., 100
Gunther, John, 40

Haldane, J.B.S., 100
Hayflick, L., 60
Herriot, James, 73
Hilton, Conrad, 39
Hippocrates, 84
Holmes, Oliver Wendell, 77
Hui-neng, 114
Huxley, A., 92

Isaacs, 35

Jacob, F., 45, 92
Jaffe, B.M., 68
Jefferson, Thomas, 82
Jesus, 117
John Paul I, 57
Johnson, Samuel, 22

DEATH

Kapitza, P., 108
Knowles, John, 35, 76
Koestler, Arthur, 40, 94, 102
Krishna, Lord, 44
Krishnamurthy, Jiddu, 108
Kübler-Ross, 86, 67, 91

Lama Anagarika Govinda, 114
Leibniz, Karl, 116
Lewis, Carl, 111
Lipkin, Mark, 49
Lorenz, Konrad, 35, 36

Malleson, A., 67
Maugham, Somerset, 111
McIntosh, 67
McKeown, T., 67
Meir, Golda, 59
Melville, Herman, 39
Montaigne, 91
Mozart, 95, 111
Munsif, 77
Murchie, G., 86

Nasser, Gamal Abdul, 53, 54
Nehru, Pandit, 35, 53, 54
Nietzsche, F., 35

Opie, L.H., 58

Paré, Ambroise, 84
Pascal, 39
Pasteur, Louis, 42, 87
Picasso, Pablo, 48
Pickering, G., 68
Plato, 95, 118
Platt, Robert, 99
Plotinus, 110, 116, 118
Pope Paul IV, 57
Portmann, A., 56
Prometheus, 18
Pythagoras, 118

Quinlan, Karen Ann, 59

Rockefeller, Nelson, 57, 58
Rutstein, D.D., 83
Ryan, Cornelius, 80

Schur, Max, 93
Schweitzer, Albert, 94, 98, 101, 102, 106
Scottish physicians' memorandum, 35, 67
Shakespeare, 102
Shaw, Bernard, 42
Simms, 59, 60
Socrates, 15, 118
Solzhenitsyn, Alexander, 87, 95, 96
Sophocles, 97
Spinoza, 21, 106
St. Francis of Assisi, 49
Stalin, Joseph, 108
Susann, Jaqueline, 61
Svetaketu, 110

Tagore, Rabindranath, 35, 49, 113, 117
Tennyson, Alfred, Lord, 118
Thierry, Charles, 73
Thomas, Lewis, 104
Thompson, Leonard, 69
Tito, 59

Van der Leeuw, G., 57
Virchow, Rudolph, 26
Voltaire, 48

Watson, Lyall, 104
Watts, Alan, 45
Weinberg, A.M., 55
White, Paul Dudley, 73
White-Lea, Aurora Lucero, 33
Whitehead, Alfred North, 104
Whitman, Walt, 118
Wordsworth, William, 118

Yutang, Lin, 97

Zumoff, B., 58

Subject Index

Aquired illness, 64
Age, 25, 31, 32, 33, 43, 60, 63, 76
Ageing, 23, 24, 25, 27, 28, 29, 31, 59, 60, 61, 71, 80, 83, 105
Aham Brahmosmi, 108-109
Anatomy of an Illness, 73
Antidiabetic agent, 72
Art of Loving, The, 91
Arteriosclerosis, 23, 71
Arthritis, 26, 48, 69, 72
Atheromatous process, 71
Atherosclerosis, 23, 60,
Autoimmune diseases, 23, 26, 29, 72
Awareness, 105, 106, 109, 111, 118

Bhagvad Gita, 103, 117, 118
Big Bang, 55, 108, 109, 114
Birth defects, 23, 30, 36, 78
Birth, 19, 24, 103, 105, 107, 109, 112, 113, 117
Blood cholesterol, 62
Blood pressure, 15, 22, 23, 25, 28, 31, 48, 61, 62, 63, 67, 68, 75, 82
Blood sugar, 25, 61
Blood vessels, 48, 51, 52, 53
Brahman, 109, 110, 111, 112, 115
Brain, 18, 19, 35, 47, 48, 50, 52, 53, 59, 62, 69, 106
Bypass, 25, 72, 82

Cancer, 16, 22, 23, 26, 28-32, 34-39, 41, 42, 49, 50, 56, 59, 60, 61, 63, 64, 67, 69, 70, 71, 72, 74, 75, 76, 78, 79, 82, 83, 87, 88, 93, 100, 109
Cardiac arrest, 52
Cataract, 24, 25, 70
Cells, 26, 27, 46, 47, 48, 51, 60, 61, 70, 71, 72, 104, 109, 115, 116
Cellularity, 70-71, 74
Cerebral hemispheres, 50

Cerebral hemorrhage, 58
Cerebrovascular disease, 68
Chemicals, anti-abnormal cell agents, 71
Chemotherapy, 82
Childhood, 19, 46
Chloroplasts, 106
Chromosomal abnormalities, 28
Circulation, system of, 50, 51
Cirrhosis of liver, 37
Cleft palate, 70, 74, 79
Collagen fibers, 23, 27, 28, 48, 56, 60, 61
Collagen, senescent, 28
Collagenous disorders, 23
Coma, 52, 119
Compassion, 78, 82, 97
Conception, 19, 22, 24, 36, 45, 46, 59
Conference, clinicopathological, 39, 50, 58
Congenital malformations, 23, 64, 67, 75, 78
Coronary angiogram, 76
Coronary artery disease (See also Heart attack) 41, 82
Coronary artery oclusion, 15, 48, 67, 72
Coronary bypass, 67, 68
Corporate, genotype, 74, 75, 78
CT scan, 69, 70, 73
Cytofiberkinetics, 27
Cytofibernetics, 27, 29, 61
Cytologic aberration, 64
Cytology, 66

Decay, 19, 116
Deformity, 82
Development, 19, 51, 56, 64, 82
Diabetes, 15, 16, 22, 23, 24, 25, 29, 31,

125

DEATH
34, 38, 46, 48, 53, 63, 67, 68, 69, 71, 72, 75, 79, 82, 88
Diabetogen, 26
Diagnosis, 15, 20, 39, 46, 66, 68, 69, 71, 73, 77,
Dictionary of Modern Thought, 78
Disease, 16, 18, 19-21, 22-23, 25-29, 30, 31, 33, 34, 37, 38, 42, 46-49, 52, 55-65, 66-77, 78-90, 109, 112
DNA, 104, 116
Doctor (See also Physician) 20, 42, 68, 69, 70, 80, 82, 83, 84, 85-90, 98, 100
Drosophila, 76

Eastern sages, 81, 105, 114
ECG, 25, 64, 73
EKG, 25, 64, 73
Embryogenesis, human, 28
Emphysema, 59
Encephalin, 42
Endocrines, 52, 53
Epidemiologist, 37, 68
Epidemiology, 69
Epistemology, 39, 69, 104
Essential hypertension, See Blood pressure
Etiology, of human malformations, 67
Euthanasia, 92, 94, 99-101
Euvivasia, 92, 94, 98, 99
Existence, 43, 94, 95, 102, 106, 110, 111, 117

Fall, The, 81

Gene pool, 29, 41
Genotype, identicality of, 72
Gera, 83
Gerontogen, 26
Gerontologists, 27
Gestational choriocarcinoma, 72
God, 95, 100, 106

Hayflick limit, 60
Heart, 51, 52, 53, 54, 113

Heart attack, 15, 16, 22, 23, 26, 28, 31, 32, 34, 37, 38, 39, 46, 48, 50, 53, 57, 58, 63, 64, 67, 69, 72, 75, 93,
Heart beat, 46, 51, 53, 54
Heart transplant, 44
Herd, 16, 19, 20, 29, 30, 31, 36, 37, 39, 41, 61, 74, 75, 76, 78, 80, 81, 82
Hernia, 70
Hodgkin's disease, 42, 49
Homeopathy, 85
Homicide, 110
Hospice movement, 98, 99
Hyperacidity, 82
Hypertensinogen, 26
Hypertension, See Blood pressure

Illness, advanced, 42, 54, 86, 87
Immortality, 44, 117
Immune system, 51
Immunization, 34
Immunotherapy, 71
Indian scriptures, 83, 89, 96, 111, 115
Individuality, 71, 116
Infancy, 19, 25
Infant mortality, 67
Infection, 31, 34, 38
Information, 107, 108, 109, 115, 116,
Inheritance, multifactorial, 30
polygenic, 75
Interactional diseases, 23, 30
Intestines, gangrene of, 48
Intrinsic diseases, 23

Janus, 94
Journal of Biological Chemistry, The, 116

Kidney failure, 46, 48

Leukemia, 24, 36, 37, 59, 74, 79
Life, 16, 34, 35, 38, 40, 45, 46, 51, 52, 56, 81, 88, 91-101, 102-112, 113-118
Life span, 24, 25, 28, 31, 38, 47, 49, 60
Logic of Living Systems, The, 45, 92

SUBJECT INDEX

Lungs, 52, 53
Lymphoma, 59

Mahabharat, 44
Malnutrition, 31
Mammals, 60, 61
Man, 18, 27, 55, 60, 65, 76, 82, 92, 103, 104, 106, 107, 108, 109, 110, 111, 117, 118
Man and Time, 56
Mankind, 16, 18, 22, 31, 37, 74, 100, 102, 103
Matter, 56, 65, 108, 115
Maturation, 19, 45, 59
Medical science, 19, 22, 27, 56, 64
Medicalization of death, 89
Medicine, 23, 25, 26, 34, 35, 37, 38, 56, 57, 58, 61, 63, 66, 67, 70, 72, 73, 77, 81, 82-85, 93
Menopause, 41
Mental retardation, 62
Mercy killing, 92, 93
Mind, 103, 105, 109, 112, 113, 117, 118
Mitochondria, 107
Moksha, 109
Molecular biology, 26, 66
Molecules, 27
Monads, 116
Mortality, 31, 36, 37, 41, 49, 58, 60, 88, 94, 119
Mouse, 60, 61
Mrutyu Upanishad, 16
Murder, 92
Mutative repertoire, 71

Natural selection, 36
Naturopathy, 85
Neocanceration, 72
Neural tube defects, 74
Nirvana, 109
Niyama, 21
Nosogen, 26
Nuclear magnetic resonance, 69

Old age, 25, 39, 81
Ontogeny, 43

Ontolysis, 43, 81
Ovum, 46

Pain, 100
Panacea, panexistential, 105
Parsis, 30, 31
Partha, 111
Past illness, 43
Pathogen, 26
Patient, 16, 17, 63, 73, 77, 82, 84, 86, 87, 88, 89, 90
Peptic Ulcer, 63, 70, 75
Perennial complex, 46, 47
Perennial Philosophy, The, 92
Peripheral artery disease, 67, 68
Physician (See also Doctor) 16, 17, 54, 69, 77, 89, 105
Physics, 74, 105, 108, 114
Physiology, 45
Pilgrim's Progress, The, 103
Pneumonia, 24, 59
Polygenes, 79
Population aggregates, 75
Porphyria, 75
Post-carnate phase, 116
Probability, 15, 63, 75
Prognosis, 25, 33, 37, 39, 56, 58, 59, 66, 68, 73
Purnamadah Purnamidam, 107-108

Race, 31, 32, 107
Rate of malformations, 67
Regeneration, 47
Reincarnation, 118
Relativity, 56, 60-61, 64, 65
Reproductive fitness, 27
Respiration, 46, 50, 60
Retinae, 70
Reye's syndrome, 119
Rigveda, 13

Sat-Chit-Ananda, 106, 111-112
Satori, 96
Science, 55, 64, 104, 105, 113, 117
Science Digest, 54
Scriptures, 16, 46, 83, 89, 91, 95, 109, 111, 115
Selection pressure, 41

DEATH

Senescence, 24, 25, 26, 27, 29, 47, 56, 59, 60, 83, 93
Senescogen, 26
Senility, 19, 26
Sensory receptors, 46
Severity of diverse diseases, 63
Sex, 31, 33, 43, 80
Shiva, 20
Silent Spring, 96
Society, 78, 80, 82, 85, 94
Space, 56, 65, 105, 108, 113, 114, 115
Species, 57, 60, 61, 63
Sperm, 46, 116
Spinal cord, tumors of, 47
Stress, 110
Stroke, 23, 26, 28, 31, 32, 38, 41, 46, 50, 67, 68, 72, 75, 78, 93
Submolecules, 27
Suicide, 92, 93, 95, 110
Supporting complex, 46, 47
Surgeon, 77, 79
Survival, 37, 40, 41, 63, 69, 89,
Symposia, 56, 67
Systemicity, 70, 71-72, 74

Tachythanasia, 93
Taoism, 20, 21, 95
Tat Twam Asi, 109-111
Technique, 66, 69
Testes, 41
Thanatognosis, 18, 20, 55, 85-90
Tibetan Book of the Dead, The, 109
Time, 19, 20, 24, 38-39, 56-60, 65, 83, 86, 89, 91, 94-95, 100, 105, 113, 115, 116, 117
Timeless Moment, This, 94
Trajectory, biological, 73
Trans-modern-medicine, 56, 64

Trans-science, 55, 64, 65
Trans-technique, 64, 66, 70, 73
Treatment, 15, 26, 33, 36, 37, 42, 66, 68, 69, 72, 73, 77, 82, 88, 89
Trimurti, 20
Tuberculosis, 22
Tumor mass, 70
Two Hands of God, The, 45

Ulcer, 63, 110
Ultrasonography, 69
Uniqueness, 70, 72-74, 114, 115, 116
Universe, 96, 97, 98, 105, 108, 113, 114, 115, 116
Uttar Ramcharit, 81

Variability, 72
Variations, quantitative, 63
Vascular diseases, 23, 31, 46
Vishnu, 20
Vyadhi, 83

Wear-and-tear theory, 27
West, 80, 82, 95, 102, 104-105
Wisdom, 89, 106, 108, 117
Womb, 19, 47, 51, 57
World population, 34, 114
Worm infestation, 30
Wrinkles, 25

X-rays, 69, 73
Xeroradiography, 69

Yama, 20, 21
Yami, 20
Yoga, 96

Zen, 45, 96
Zygote, 46, 56